The Guide To The Koine Greek New Testament

Hazel S. Lee

Introduction

This is a comprehensive guide that delves into the study of the Koine Greek language, with a specific focus on its application to the New Testament texts. The book covers various aspects of Koine Greek, including its alphabet, grammar, and verb forms, providing readers with the foundational knowledge required to read and understand New Testament texts in their original language.

The book begins by introducing readers to the Greek language and its alphabet, laying the groundwork for further exploration. It then proceeds to cover the present indicative tense, which is a crucial verb form in Koine Greek.

The declensions of second and first declension nouns are discussed in detail, along with their various cases and the definite article. Neuter nouns of the second declension are also examined.

First declension feminine nouns with different endings and masculine nouns are introduced, along with more information on noun cases. The book proceeds to cover adjectives of the second declension and their usage, as well as the verb "to be."

Verbs in the imperfect and compound forms are explained, followed by a discussion of demonstratives and various pronouns, including personal, possessive, and reflexive pronouns.

Time expressions and prepositions are explored, and the passive voice in Greek is discussed in depth. The book also delves into the relative pronoun and the present imperative.

Different types of pronouns, including αυτος, εαυτον, αλλος, and αλληλους, are covered, along with the use of δυναμαι and the infinitive. The future tense and the stem of a verb are also explained.

The middle voice and the future of ειμι are discussed, as well as the future and aorist of liquid verbs and the word οτι. The first and second aorist middle forms are also explained.

The book covers the third declension and its neuter nouns, along with third declension adjectives, interrogative, and indefinite pronouns. Adjectives and pronouns with first and third declensions are also examined, along with forms for comparison.

The perfect and pluperfect tenses are discussed, along with the aorist and future passives. More advanced topics, such as the genitive absolute and periphrastic tenses, are also covered.

The subjunctive mood and the optative mood are explained, providing readers with a comprehensive understanding of verb forms and moods in Koine Greek.

Overall, this book serves as an expert guide for individuals interested in studying the Greek language and its application to the New Testament texts. The book offers a thorough exploration of grammar, verb forms, and other essential components of the language, equipping readers with the knowledge necessary to engage with New Testament texts in their original language.

Contents

The Greek Language and Alphabet

Greek is a language with a long history. It can be traced back as far as the 13th century BC when it had a form known as Linear B. The more ancient forms have been preserved in the writings of Homer and Hesiod (8th century BC) and later with Plato (4th century BC). Greek came onto the world stage with the conquests of Alexander the Great. He and his generals brought the dialect of Attic Greek with them and it quickly became the common,'koine', language of its day. This Koine Greek would be used by Jewish translators who rendered the Old Testament from Hebrew into Greek in the 2nd and 3rd centuries BC.

In the time of Christ even though the Roman empire had dominance in the region the apostles would communicate to each other through their letters and gospels in Greek and not Latin (even the letter to the Romans was written in Greek). Greek would later become the official language of the Byzantine empire, the Eastern side of the Roman empire. Today Greek is very much a living language in Greece, although its modern form is quite different.

Alphabet

The Greek alphabet is based on the Phoenician, from which Hebrew and Latin also have their origins. There are a total of 24 letters in Greek, which are given in the following table. In the time of the apostles only the capital letters were used, and the earliest manuscripts only have these. However later the small letters were used, because they could be written cursively.

A number of different possible pronunciation schemes have been put forth for ancient Greek. Here we provide the modern Greek pronunciation. Although it is not necessary for reading the language it can help with remembering the words and allows one to potentially interact with modern Greeks.

Greek Alphabet

α	A	a	a as in father
β	B	b	v as in vote
γ	Γ	g	g as in get
δ	Δ	d	'th' as in there
ε	E	e	e as in pet
ζ	Z	z	z as in zoo
η	H	e	ee as in greet
θ	Θ	th	th as in thin
ι	I	i	ee as in greet
κ	K	k	ck as in pack
λ	Λ	l	l as in like
μ	M	m	m as in move
ν	N	n	n as in note
ξ	Ξ	x	x as in axe
o	O	o	o as in wrote
π	Π	p	p as in pat

ρ	P	r	r as in rat
σ/ ς	Σ	s	s as soak
τ	T	t	t as in stop
υ	Y	u	oo as in took
φ	Φ	ph	ph or f as in phone
χ	X	ch	ch as in loch
ψ	Ψ	ps	ps as in lips
ω	Ω	o	o as in boat

Diphthongs and Special Groups

Certain combinations of letters are referred to as diphthongs and are given in the table below:

Diphthongs

αι	e as in bet
ει	ee as in feet
οι	ee as in feet
υι	ee as in feet
ου	oo as in pool
αυ	'af' before (π,κ,τ,φ,χ,θ,σ,ξ,ψ) and 'av' elsewhere
ευ	'ef' before (π,κ,τ,φ,χ,θ,σ,ξ,ψ) and 'ev' elsewhere
ηυ	'iyf' before

(π,κ,τ,φ,χ,θ,σ,ξ,ψ)
and 'iyv' elsewhere

In addition to the diphthongs the following combinations of letters alter the pronunciation.

γγ / γκ	ng as in finger
γξ	nks as in banks
μπ	mb sound
ντ	nd sound

The Iota Subscript and Accents

The small ι, is sometimes written underneath vowels:ᾳ,ῃ or ῳ. This does not affect the pronunciation.

All Greek words starting with a vowel have a 'breathing' mark above them. Diphthongs have their mark on the second vowel. There are two forms of the marks: rough "'" (ἁ) or smooth "'" (ἀ). Again these do not affect the pronunciation of the word.

There are additional accents, which can change the meaning of a word. But this is rare, and generally accents can be ignored, since accents only indicate which syllable is stressed in speach.

Note: If a word ending in a vowel is followed by another word starting with a vowel or diphthong, the last letter is 'elided' or dropped out. so δια → δι' or αλλα → αλλ'

Note: The punctuation of Greek is largely the same as English except ';' is a question mark.

Exercises

1) Write out each letter from Table 1 to become comfortable with the form.

2) The following verse is John 1:1,2 and includes all the accents. Copy out the verse and try to pronounce it. 1 Ἐν ἀρχῇ ἦν ὁ Λόγος, καὶ ὁ Λόγος ἦν πρὸς τὸν Θεόν, καὶ Θεὸς ἦν ὁ Λόγος. 2 Οὗτος ἦν ἐν ἀρχῇ πρὸς τὸν Θεόν.

The Present Indicative

The most basic sentence one can write in English consists of a subject and verb, e.g. "I go". For ancient Greek the most basic example uses the verb "loose" (λυ-).

To write "I loose", "you loose", etc., the subjects (I,you, he/she/it) are added to a stem of the verb. The standard example is λυ-:

Conjugation of λυω

1st person	Singular	λυω	I loose
2nd person	Singular	λυεις	you loose
3rd person	Singular	λυει	he looses
1st person	Plural	λυομεν	we loose
2nd person	Plural	λυετε	you (pl) loose
3rd person	Plural	λυουσι(ν)	they loose

Note:

- All of the verbs could be alternatively translated as "I am loosing; you are loosing; etc." Although more awkward, this gives perhaps a closer sense of the present tense in the Greek which is a continuous form.

- In ancient Greek the pronoun (I, you, he, etc.) is not necessary since it is built into the verb forms.
- The 3rd person plural has a "movable ν" which may or may not be present, depending on the word that follows it.

In order to reinforce the material presented here and in later lessons, exercises are placed at the end of each lesson. The reader is encouraged to translate the English to Greek and then to go through translating the Greek to English. It is important to resist looking at the answer and to work through all the exercises first.

There will also be a vocabulary section at the end of most lessons which contains words frequently found in the New Testament. Verbs are listed in the first person singular form.

Exercises

1. We loose
2. They loose.
3. We judge
4. Are you (pl.) writing?
5. He is sending.

1. λυομεν
2. λυουσιν
3. κρινομεν
4. γραφετε;
5. πεμπει

Vocabulary

βαλλω	I throw
βλεπω	I see
γινωσκω	I know
εχω	I have
θεραπευω	I heal
κρινω	I judge
λαμβανω	I take
λεγω	I say
λυω	I loose.
μενω	I remain
πεμπω	I send.
σωζω	I save.

-εω verbs

Verbs that end in –εω can contract when endings are added to their stems. These contractions take place according to the following rules:

1. ε + ε → ει
2. ε + ο → ου
3. ε + long vowel or diphthong → long vowel or diphthong

φιλεω (I love) is conjugated as:

Conjugation of φιλεω

Contracted	Uncontracted	Translation
φιλω	φιλεω	I love
φιλεις	φιλεεις	you love
φιλει	φιλεει	he loves
φιλουμεν	φιλεομεν	we love
φιλειτε	φιλεετε	you (pl.) love
φιλουσι(ν)	φιλεουσι(ν)	they love

Exercises

1. They are seeking
2. he asks
3. you call
4. we are bearing witness
5. I speak

1. λεγουσιν

2. αιτει
3. καλεις
4. μαρτυρυομεν
5. λαλω

Vocabulary

βλασφημεω	I blaspheme
ευλογεω	I bless [eulogise]
καλεω	I call
λαλεω	I speak
μαρτυρεω	I bear witness [martyr]
μετανοεω	I repent
μισεω	I hate
ποιεω	I do
τηρεω	I keep
φιλεω	I love
ζητεω	I seek
θεωρεω	I look at

Second Declension Nouns in –ος and Cases

Nouns are inflected based on their case (subject, object, etc.) and do not have an indefinite article. The declension of the word λογος is given in the table below.

Note: We use the short forms: sg. (singular), pl. (plural), subj. (subject) and obj. (object).

Declension of λογος

Nominative (N) sg.	λογος	a word (sub.)
Vocative (V) sg.	λογε	O word
Accusative (A) sg.	λογον	a word (obj.)
Genitive (G) sg.	λογου	of a word
Dative (D) sg.	λογῳ	to or for a word
Nominative (N) pl.	λογοι	words (sub.)
Vocative (V) pl.	λογοι	O words
Accusative (A) pl.	λογους	words (obj.)
Genitive (G) pl.	λογων	of words
Dative (D) pl.	λογοις	to or for words

In English the position of the noun in the sentence relates to the case, that is, "a man teaches a child" has a different meaning than the sentence, "a child teaches a man", because the subject ("man") and object ("child") have been switched. However in Greek the position of the noun does not define the case, but instead how it is declined. So "ανθροπος διδασκει τεκνον" and "διδασκει τεκνον ανθροπος" have the same meaning.

Some verbs (such as μενω, I remain) cannot have a direct object. These are known as *intransitive* verbs. A verb may function in a intransitive (e.g. I stop) or transitive (e.g. I stop the man) manner.

The verb should agree in number with its subject. e.g ανθρωποι εγειρουσιν λιθον: the men raise a stone

A noun in the vocative case sometimes is preceded by ω meaning "O".

Example:

Κυριε Ιησου Χριστε σωζεις : Lord Jesus Christ, you save.

ω Κυριε Ιησου Χριστε σωζεις : O Lord Jesus Christ, you save.

Exercises

1. An angel calls a man.
2. A brother has a field.
3. Lords send messengers.
4. They are writing words.
5. Are you (pl.) finding a stone?
6. Christ judges men and angels.

1. αγγελος καλει ανθροπον.
2. αδελφος εχει αγρος.

3. κυριοι πεμπουσιν αγγελους.
4. λογους γραφουσιν.
5. ευρισκετε λιθον.
6. Χριστος κρινει ανθρωπους και αγγελους.

Vocabulary

ω	O!
και	and, even, also
Ισραηλ	Israel
Ιουδαιος	Jew
Φαρισαιος	Pharisee
Χριστος	Christ
αγγελος	messenger
αγρος	field
αδελφος	brother
ανθρωπος	man
αποστολος	apostle
διακονος	servant, deacon
διδασκαλος	teacher
εχθρος	enemy
θανατος	death
θρονος	throne
κοσμος	world
κυριος	lord
λαος	people
λεπρος	leper

λιθος	stone
λογος	word
νομος	law
οφθαλμος	eye
παραλυτικος	paralytic
ποταμος	river
πρεσβυτερος	presbyter, elder
τοπος	place
φιλος	friend
φοβος	fear

More on Cases and the Definite Article

The Dative Case

One could think of an arrow pointing from the verb to the direct object in this case, which generally implies something done "to" or "for" the object.

πεμπει οινον τεκνω : 1) He sends wine to a child. *or* 2) He sends wine for a child.

The Genitive Case

The genitive case implies ownership which we could translate one of two ways in English:

λιθος τεκνου : 1) A stone of a child *or* 2) A child's stone.

The Definite Article

The article "the" must match the case of the noun and is declined as follows:

The definite article for masculine nouns*

Singular	
N	o

A	τον
G	του
D	τῳ
Plural	
N	οι
A	τους
G	των
D	τοις

* here we have used the short form N/A/G/D which stand for the nominative, associative, genitive and dative cases.

Note: The endings are the same as λογος.

There are some situations in which the article is used in Greek where it would not appear in English:

1. Θεος: Ο Υιος του Θεος (The son of God)
2. With abstract noun such as ανθρωπος, which refer to a whole class: ο υιος του ανθρωπου (The son of man)
3. With certain names such as Ιησους, although it depends on the author. There is no set rule for this.

When the verb "to be" is used both the object and the subject appear in the nominative form so the meaning may not be clear:

ο Λογος εστιν ο Θεος: The word is God **or** God is the word.

To make this clearer the object generally drops the article:

Θεος εστιν ο Λογος : The word is God.

Note: Ιησους has an irregular declination:

Jesus

N.	Ιησους
A.	Ιησουν
G.V.D.	Ιησου

Exercises

1. Does time remain?
2. Are you (pl.) seeking the heavens?
3. James has a reward for the son.
4. We see a desert.
5. The angel writes laws for the world.
6. The man's slave is making bread.
7. The devil seeks a time for Christ's temptations.
8. Sinners see the apostle's words and repent.

1. χρονος μενει;
2. ζητειτε τους ουρανους;
3. Ιακωβος εχει μισθον τω υιω.
4. βλεπομεν ερημον.
5. ο αγγελος γραφει νομους τω κοσμω.
6. ο δουλος του ανθρωπου ποιει αρτον.
7. ο διαβολος ζητει καιρον τοις πειρασμοις του Χηριστου.
8. αμαρταλοι βλεπουσιν τους των αποστολων λογους και
μετανοουσιν.

Vocabulary

εστιν	is
Ιησους	Jesus
Ιακωβος	James
αμαρτωλος	sinner
ανεμος	wind
αρτος	bread
διαβολος	devil
δουλος	slave
ηλιος	Sun
θεος	God
καρπος	fruit
μισθος	reward, pay
ναος	temple
οικος	house
οινος	wine
ουρανος	heaven
οχλος	crowd
πειρασμος	temptation
σταυρος	cross
υιος	son
καιρος	fitting season, opportunity, time
χρονος	time
ερημος	desert (fem.)
οδος	way (fem.)
παρθενος	virgin (fem.)
αιτεω	I ask

Second Declension – Neuter Nouns

Nouns may be either, masculine, feminine or neuter. One can often infer the gender based on the ending of the noun. Generally nouns in the nominative form ending in –ος are masculine, and they belong to the second declension. Neuter nouns end in –ον and are also part of the 2nd declension.

The noun εγρον (work) is declined as:

Declension of εγρον

+	Singular	Plural
N	εργον	εργα
V	εργον	εργα
A	εργον	εργα
G	εργου	εργων
D	εργω	εργοις

Like the masculine form, the definite article (the) has the same endings as the –ον noun:

The Neuter Definite Article

+	Singular	Plural
N	τον	τα
A	τον	τα
G	του	των

D	τω		τοις	

One of the oddities of neuter nouns is that they do not always agree in number with the verb. Generally the singular verb is used with plural neuter nouns.

τα τεκνα πεμπει αρτους : The children send bread.

Exercises

1. Christ blesses the cup of wine and the bread.
2. Do you know the signs of the Son of Man?
3. The Lord saves men and children.
4. The children ask the elders for garments.
5. Do you see the sheep?
6. We bear witness to the gospel of God.
7. The Jews love the Sabbath and Jerusalem.
8. Angles see the face of God.

1. Χριστος ευλογει το ποτηριον του οικου και τον αργον.
2. γινωσκεις τα σημεια του Υιου του ανθρωπου;
3. ο κυριος σωζει τους ανθρωπους και τα τεκνα.
4. Τα τεκνα αιτει τους πρεσβυτερους ιματια.
5. βλεπεις τα προβατα;
6. μαρτυρουμεν τω ευαγγελιω του Θεου.
7. οι Ιουδαιοι φιλει το σαββατον και τα Ιεροσολυμα.
8. αγγελλοι θευρουσιν το προσωπον του Θεου.

Vocabulary

αργυριον	silver, money
βιβλιον	book

δαιμονιον	demon
δενδρον	tree
εργον	work
ευαγγελιον	gospel
ιερον	temple
ιματιον	garment; clothes
μνημειον	tomb
μυστηριον	mystery
παιδιον	child
τεκνον	child
πλοιον	boat
ποτηριον	cup
προβατον	sheep
προσωπον	face
σημειον	sign
συνεδριον	council, Sanhedrin
σαββατον	Sabbath
Ιεροσολυμα	Jerusalem

First Declension Feminine Nouns Ending in – η

There are three forms of feminine nouns, all of which belong to the first declension:

1. Feminine nouns ending in –η.
2. Feminine nouns ending in –α.
3. Masculine nouns ending in –ης or -α.

In this chapter we focus on the first category with the noun αρχη which has the declination:

Declension αρχη

+	Singular	Plural
N.V.	αρχη	αρχαι
A	αρχην	αρχας
G	αρχης	αρχων
D	αρχη	αρχαις

The definite article (the) which accompanies all feminine nouns is declined as:

The feminine definite article

+	Singular	Plural
N	η	αι
A	την	τας
G	της	των

D	τη	ταις

Exercises

1. God is judging the earth.
2. You know the commandments.
3. The apostles love God's covenant.
4. He has money, the price of a field.
5. The elders of the village throw stones.
6. God saves men's souls.
7. James sends a letter for the apostle's friend.

1. ο θεος κρινει την γην.
2. γινωσκετε τας εντολας.
3. οι αποστολοι φιλουσιν την του Θεου διαθηκην.
4. εχει αργυριον, την τιμην αγρου.
5. οι πρεσβυτεροι της κωμης βαλλουσιν λιθους.
6. ο Θεος σωζει τας ψυχας των ανθρωπων.
7. Ιακωβος πεμπει επιστολη τω φιλω αποστολου.

Vocabulary

αγαπη	love
αρχη	beginning
γη	earth
γραφη	writing
διαθηκη	covenant
διδαχη	teaching
δικαιοσυνη	righteousness
ειρηνη	peace
εντολη	commandment

επιστολη	letter
ζωη	life
κεφαλη	head
κωμη	village
νεφελη	cloud
οργη	anger
παραβολη	parable
προσευχη	prayer
συναγωγη	synagogue
τιμη	honour, price
υπομονη	steadfastness
φυλακη	guard, prison
φωνη	sound, voice
ψυχη	soul, life

First Declension Feminine Nouns Ending in – α

The second group of feminine nouns have slightly different declensions in the singular.

The declension of ημερα (day) is,

Declension of ημερα

+	Singular	Plural
N.V.	ημερα	ημεραι
A	ημεραν	ημερας
G	ημερας	ημερων
D	ημερα	ημεραις

while δοξα (glory) is,

Declension of δοξα

+	Singular	Plural
N.V.	δοξα	δοξαι
A	δοξαν	δοξας
G	δοξης	δοξων
D	δοξη	δοξαις

Note:

- The plural endings are the same.
- αρχη και ημερα have the same endings except that η is replaced with α in genitive and dative.
- When the stem of the noun ends with a vowel or ρ then it follows the declension of ημερα.

Exercises

1. They seek the time of the promise.
2. The angels of heaven have joy.
3. Paul bears witness to the truth of the gospel and the wisdom of God.
4. Repentance is the door of salvation.
5. Do the children repent?
6. The door of the tomb is a stone.
7. God makes the seas, the rocks of the earth and the clouds of heaven.
8. The need of the widow is joy.
9. Christ has the authority of God.

1. ζητουσιν τον καιρον της επαγγελιας.
2. οι αγγελοι των ουρανων εχουσιν την χαραν.
3. ο Παυλος μαρτυρει τη αληθεια του ευαγγελιου και τη σοφια του Θεου.
4. η μετανοια εστιν θυρα της σωτεριας.
5. τα παιδια μετανοει;
6. η θυρα του μνημιου εστιν λιθος.
7. ο Θεος ποιει τας θαλασσας, τας πετρας της γης και τας νεφελας τνω ουρανων.
8. η χρηια της χηρας χαρα εστιν.
9. Χριστος εχει την εξουσιαν του Θεου.

Vocabulary

αδικια	unrighteousness
αληθεια	truth
αμαρτια	sin
βασιλεια	kingdom, sovereignty, royal rule
γενεα	generation
εκκλησια	assembly, congregation, church.
εξουσια	authority
επαγγελια	promise
ημερα	day
θυρα	door
θυσια	sacrifice
καρδια	heart
μαρτυρια	witness
μετανοια	repentance
οικια	house
παρουσια	coming
πετρα	rock
σοφια	wisdom
σωτηρια	salvation
χαρα	joy
χηρα	widow
χρεια	need
ωρα	hour
Γαλιλαια	Galilee
Ιουδαια	Judaea
γλωσσα	tongue
δοξα	glory

θαλασσα	sea
Παυλος	Paul
Πετρος	Peter

First Declension Masculine Nouns and More on Cases

Masculine nouns of the 1st declension end in –ης or –ας. The declension of προφητης (prophet) is,

Declension of προφητης

+	Singular	Plural
N	προφητης	προφηται
V	προφητα	προφηται
A	προφητην	προφητας
G	προφητου	προφητων
D	προφητη	προφηταις

while νεανιας (young man) is,

Declension of νεανιας

+	Singular	Plural
N	νεανιας	νεανιαι
V	νεανια	νεανιαι
A	νεανιαν	νεανιας
G	νεανιου	νεανιων
D	νεανια	νεανιαις

Note:

1. Only the vocative (V) and genitive (G) differ from the feminine nouns.

2. Since these nouns are masculine they will take a masculine article.

Nouns of the first declension with endings -ας are usually proper names (Ανδρεας or Ηλειας). The genitive endings when the stem ends with ε,ι, or ρ are -ου, but with other letters (Σατανας or Ιουδας) they have "Doric" genitive endings -α.

The Accusative

This is the case used for the direct object; however when it is used with a preposition its meaning involves one of motion. In particular, with εις, the meaning is "to" or "into". Similarly with προς the meaning is "to" or "towards".

The Genitive

This case refers to the possession of something ("the book of the child"). More generally the genitive indicates "a kind" of something. When used with prepositions then its meaning shifts to one of removal or separation. Examples would be:

απο + gen. : from / away from

εκ + gen. : out of / from

The Dative

The dative is used for indirect objects that are "to" or "for" something or someone. When used with prepositions it has a "locative" sense:

εν + dat. : in

It can also indicate the object which has an "instrumental" role in the sentence:

ο αποστολος σωζει φιλον επιστολη : the apostle saves a friend by a letter

Exercises

1. Jesus therefore says, 'The Son of man is in the clouds of the heavens.'
2. The Jews seek the prophet's voice in the desert.
3. Do the sons of God keep the commandments out of the heart?
4. Do the tax-collectors blaspheme?
5. The disciples then have the love of God.
6. The workmen do not find the way to the cross, and they do not see the sacrifice of Jesus.
7. Christ speaks the parables to the young men; for they seek the truth.

1. Λεγει ουν ο Ιησους, 'Ο Υιος του ανθρωπου εστιν εν ταις νεφελαις των ουρανων.
2. οι Ιουδαιοι ζητουσιν την φωνην του προφητου εν τη ερημω.
3. οι υιοι των ανθρωπων τηρουσιν τας εντολας εκ καρδιας;
4. οι τελωναι βλασφημουσιν;
5. οι αρα μαθηται εχει την αγαπην του Θεου.

6. οι εργαται ουχ ευρισκουσιν τον οδον εις τον σταυρον, και την θυσιαν του Ιησου ου θεωρουσιν.
7. Χριστος λαλει εν αραβολαις τοις νεανιαις, ζητουσιν γαρ την αληθιαν.

Vocabulary

Ιωανης	John
βαπτιστης	baptist
έργατης	workman
κριτης	judge
μαθητης	disciple
προφητης	prophet
στρατιωτης	soldier
τελωνης	Tax-collector
υποκριτης	hypocrite
νεανιας	young man
Ανδρεας	Andrew
Ηλειας	Elijah
Σατανας	Satan
Ιουδας	Judas
to,into	προς
to,towards	απο
from	εκ
from, out of	αλλα
but	γαρ
for	ουν
therefore, then	δε

but	ουδε
and not, not even	αρα

Adjectives of the Second Declension and their Use

Like nouns, adjectives have a number (singular / plural), gender (masculine, feminine, neuter) and case (nominative, vocative, associative, genitive, dative) . Only the feminine declension differs if the stem ends in a ρ or a vowel. The adjective αγαθος (good) is declined as,

Declension of αγαθος

		Mas.	Fem.	Neu.
Singular	N	αγαθος	αγαθη	αγαθον
	V	αγαθε	αγαθη	αγαθον
	A	αγαθον	αγαθην	αγαθον
	G	αγαθου	αγαθης	αγαθου
	D	αγαθω	αγαθη	αγαθω
Plural	N.V.	αγαθοι	αγαθαι	αγαθα
	A	αγαθους	αγαθας	αγαθα
	G	αγαθων	αγαθων	αγαθων
	D	αγαθοις	αγαθαις	αγαθοις

while αγιος (holy) is declined as,

Declension of αγιος

		Mas.	Fem.	Neu.
Singular	N	αγιος	αγια	αγιον

	V	αγιοε	αγια	αγιον
	A	αγιον	αγιαν	αγιον
	G	αγιου	αγιας	αγιου
	D	αγιω	αγια	αγιω
Plural	N.V.	αγιοι	αγιαι	αγια
	A	αγιους	αγιας	αγια
	G	αγιων	αγιων	αγιων
	D	αγιοις	αγιαις	αγιοις

Use of Adjectives

When there is no definite article the adjective can come before or after the noun:

αγαθος αποστολος / αποστολος αγαθος : a good apostle

When a definite article is present the adjective is put in the "attributive position", which has two forms:

ο αγαθος αποστολος / ο αποστολος ο αγαθος : the good apostle.

As in English, adjectives can also be used as nouns,

ο πρωτος : the first man

αι αγαθαι : the good women

οι αγιοι : the holy men

τα εσχατα : the last things

Exercises

1. The rest find the only young man in the desert.
2. The bad prophets do not bear witness to the truth.
3. The soldiers first make a new cross for the Son of God.
4. Good words save men from death.
5. Does Paul remain faithful?
6. Andrew is Christ's first apostle.

1. οι λοιποι ευρισκουσιν τον μονον νεανιαν εν τη ερημω.
2. οι κακοι προφηται ου μαρτυρουσιν τη αληθεια.
3. οι στρατιωται πρωτον ποιουσιν νεον σταυρον τω Υιω του Θεου.
4. Αγαθοι λογοι σωζουσιν ανθρωπους εκ του θανατου.
5. Παυλος μενει πιστος;
6. ο Ανδρεας πρωτος μαθητης του Χριστου εστιν.

Vocabulary

αγαθος	good
αγαπητος	beloved
δυνατος	powerful, possible
εκαστος	each, every
εσχατος	last
ικανος	sufficient
καινος	new
κακος	bad
καλος	beautiful, good
λοιπος	remaining, the rest
μεσος	middle

μονος	alone, only
ολιγος	little, few
πιστος	believing, faithful
πρωτος	first
τριτος	third
πτωχος	poor
σοφος	wise
τυφλος	blind
απιστος*	unbelieving, faithless
ακαθαρτος*	unclean
αιωνιος*	eternal, everlasting

*The last three words use λογος endings for the feminine.

More on Adjectives and the verb "to be"

The verb "to be" is conjugated as:

Conjugation of ειμι

ειμι	I am	εσμεν	we are
εῖ	you are	εστε	you (pl) are
εστιν	he/she/it is	εισι(v)	they are

the second person singular uses an accent to distinguish it from the word "if" (εἰ).

Example: εἰ αποστολος εῖ : If you are an apostle.

The verb ειμι can also be used with an adjective as a complement

Example: ο αποστολος εστιν αγαθος / αγατος εστιν ο αποστολος : The apostle is good.

Note: that ειμι is not necessary in the above example and can be dropped.

In general, the adjective can be present in two possible positions, the attributive and predicative.

Attributive Position

Here the adjective is placed between the article and the noun or it may follow the noun with an additional article.

Example: ο αγαθος αποστολος / ο αποστολος ο αγαθος : The good apostle.

Predicative Position

In this case the adjective is placed outside of the article-noun pair and verb ειμι is dropped.

Example:αγαθος ο αποστολος / ο αποστολος αγαθος : The apostle is good.

Note: In the exercises when particles ουν, δε or γαρ are used, they will never appear as the first word and instead will usually be placed second.

Exercises

1. Elijah's servant sees a small cloud in the heavens.
2. Are you worthy?
3. The enemies of Christ are children of the devil.
4. You are the Christ.
5. The evil see the second death, for they do not love the wisdom of God.
6. Few find the way of life.
7. The old wine is good, but the new is bad.
8. The strong man looses the slave from prison.
9. We are like sheep.
10. Is it a different tomb?

1. ο διακονος του Ήλειου βλεπει μικραν νεφελην εν τοις ουρανοις.
2. εἶ αχιος;
3. εχλροι του Χριστου εισιν τεκνα του διαβολου.
4. εἶ ο Χριστος.
5. οι πονηροι βλεπουσιν τον δευτερον θανατον, ου γαρ φιλουσιν την σοφιαν του Θεου.
6. ολιγοι ευρισκουσιν την οδον της ζωης.
7. ο παλαιος οινος εστιν αγαθος, ο δε νεος εστιν κακος.
8. ο ισχυρος λυει τον δουλον εκ της φυλακης.
9. εσμεν ομοιοι προβατοις.
10. εστιν ετερον μνημειον;

Vocabulary

αγιος	holy
αξιος	worthy
δευτερος	second
δικαιος	just, righteous
ελευθερος	free
ετερος	different, other
ιδιος	one's own
ισχυρος	strong
καθαρος	clean, pure
μακαριος	happy, blessed
μικρος	small
νεκρος	dead
νεος	new, young
παλαιος	old
πλουσιος	rich
πονηρος	evil

ομοιος	like
ειμι	I am
δεξιος	right, not left.

Imperfect and Compound Verbs

The imperfect Indicative Active of λυω is:

Imperfect of λυω

ελυον	I was loosing
ελυες	You were loosing
ελυε(v)	He/she/it was loosing
ελυομεν	We were loosing
ελυετε	You (pl) were loosing
ελυον	They were loosing

The imperfect is a continuous past tense and could also be translated as: 'I used to loose', 'You used to loose', etc.

It will be noticed that this tense not only has endings after the stem, it also has an augment ε in front.

The rules of contraction are applied to -εω verbs which gives:

εφιλεον → εφιλουν

εφιλεες → εφιλεις

εφιλεε → εφιλει

εφιλεομεν → εφιλουμεν

εφιλεετε → εφιλειτε

εφιλεον → εφιλουν

If the verb begins with a vowel then the initial vowels are lengthened as follows:

α → η, ε → η, ο → ω

αι → ῃ, ει → ῃ, οι → ῳ

αυ →-ηυ, ευ → ηυ

Examples

ακουω → ηκουον

εγειρω → ηγειρον

αιτεω → ητουν

Irregular: εχω → ειχον

The meaning of the imperfect is continuous or repeated like the present. However often the simple past tense will suffice for the meaning. E.g. 'I walked' rather than 'I was walking'.

Compound Verbs

Like Greek, compound verbs are common in English:
Overheat,**under**throw and **over**hear.
Greek Examples:

αγω – I lead

απαγω – I lead away

Note that with απαγω, the original meaning is simply augmented in the compound form. However in some cases the meaning is intensified, e.g. λυω (I loose) and απολυω (I release). In other cases the meaning of the verbs is completely changed, e.g. γινωσκω (I know), but αναγινωσκω (I read).

When compound verbs are in the imperfect tense, the augment falls in between the preposition and verb, then contractions take place:

Examples:

εκβαλλω → εξεβαλλον

απαγω → απηγον

Exception: περιπατεω → περιεπατουν

Exercises

1. They were teaching the gospel to the disciples.
2. The virgins were departing from the house.

3. He was pursuing the unbelieving widow.
4. Jesus was opening the eyes of the blind, and they were recognizing their own friends.
5. You were releasing the slaves.

1. εδιδασκον τον ευαγγελιον τοις μαθηταις.
2. αι παρθενοι υπηγον απο του οικου.
3. εδιωκεν την απιστον χηραν.
4. Ιησους ωνοιγεν τους οφθαλμους των τυφλων, και επεγινωσκον τους ιδιους φιλους.
5. ελυες τους δουλους.

Vocabulary

αγω	I lead
απαγω	I lead away
συναγω	I bring or gather
υπαγω	I depart
φερω	I carry
προσφερω	I bring, offer
ακουω	I hear
υπακουω	I obey
αναγινωσκω	I read
επιγινωσκω	I perceive
αποθνησκω	I die
απολυω	I release
εκβαλλω	I throw out
ενδυω	I put on
παραλαμβανω	I receive
ανοιγω	I open

διδασκω	I teach
διωκω	I pursue
κλαιω	I weep
πειθω	I persuade
περισσευω	I abound
πιστευω	I believe
προφητευω	I prophesy
χαιρω	I rejoice

Demonstratives

The demonstratives, ουτος (this) and εκεινος (that) can be used as pronouns or adjectives.

Εκεινος is declined as:

Declencion of εκεινος

		M	F	N
Singular	N	εκεινος	εκεινη	εκεινο
	A	εκεινον	εκεινην	εκεινο
	G	εκεινου	εκεινης	εκεινου
	D	εκεινω	εκεινη	εκεινω
Plural	N	εκεινοι	εκειναι	εκεινα
	A	εκεινους	εκεινας	εκεινα
	G	εκεινων	εκεινων	εκεινων
	D	εκεινοις	εκειναις	εκεινοις

Note that the endings are the same as the articles with the exception of neuter (N) singular N/A.

ουτος is declined as:

Declencion of ουτος

		M	F	N
Singular	N	ουτος	αυτη	τουτο
	A	τουτον	ταυτην	τουτο
	G	τουτου	ταυτης	τουτου

	D	τουτω	ταυτη	τουτω
Plural	N	ουτοι	αυται	τουτα
	A	τουτους	ταυτας	ταυτα
	G	τουτων	τουτων	τουτων
	D	τουτοις	ταυταις	τουτοις

Note:

1. The endings of ουτος and εκεινος are the same.
2. The initial sounds are the same as the definite articles.
3. If the ending has an 'o' (or ω, which is a lengthened o) then the stem also does.

Unlike English, Greek uses the definite article with demonstratives:

For example: This sheep would be either: τουτο το προβατον / το προβατον τουτο

The sentence "This is the sheep" would require ειμι: τουτο εστιν το προβατον.

Note: A demonstrative can be used alone: εκεινη (that woman) **or** ταυτα (these things).

ολος, means whole and is used like a demonstrative, but it has a regular declination:

The whole sheep can be stated as either: ολον το προβατον / το προβατον ολον.

Exercises

1. This woman was following the young man.
2. That evil servant used to bind his own son.
3. These elders seem blind.
4. The happy elder was calling to the whole crowd.
5. This second brother therefore used to serve and worship God in a different temple.

1. ταυτη ηκολουυει τω νεανια.
2. εκεινος ο πονηρος διακονος εδει τον ιδιον υιον.
3. ουτοι οι πρεσβυτεροι δοκουσιν τυφλοι.
4. ο μαρκαριος πρεσβυτερος εκαλει ολον τον οχλον.
5. ουτος ουν ο δευτερος αδελφος εδιακονει και προσεκυνει τον Θεον εν ετερω ιερω.

Vocabulary

κατοικεω	I dwell
παρακαλεω	I beseech, exhort, encourage
περιπατεω	I walk
προσκυνεω	I worship
αδικεω	I do wrong to, injure
ακολουθεω	I follow
ασθενεω	I am weak/ill
γαμεω	I marry
δεω	I bind
διακονεω	I serve

δοκεω	I think, seem
ελεεω	I have mercy on
ευχαριστεω	I give thanks
κρατεω	I take hold of
οικοδομεω	I build
φωνεω	I call
ουτος	this
εκεινος	that
ολος	whole

Pronouns (αυτος, εαυτον, αλλος, αλληλους) and the Imperfect of ειμι

The 3rd person (he/she/it) αυτος is declined like εκεινος

Declension of αυτος

		M	F	N
Singular	N	αυτος	αυτη	αυτο
	A	αυτον	αυτην	αυτο
	G	αυτου	αυτης	αυτου
	D	αυτω	αυτη	αυτω
Plural	N	αυτοι	αυται	αυτα
	A	αυτους	αυτας	αυτα
	G	αυτων	αυτων	αυτων
	D	αυτοις	αυταις	αυτοις

αυτος can act as a:

1. Personal Pronoun: αυτος εσθιει τον αρτον (he eats breads). But of course the pronoun in this case is unnecessary since the sentence, εσθιει τον αρτον, has the same meaning.
2. For emphases: αυτος ο Χριστος / ο Χριστος αυτος (Christ himself). In this case the pronoun is in the predicative position.
3. As an identical adjective: ο αυτος Χριστος / ο Χριστος ο αυτος (The same Christ), in which case αυτος is in the attributive position.

The reflexive pronoun εαυτον refers back to the subject, and as a result is never found in the nominative (N):

Declension of εαυτον

A	εαυτον	εαυτην	εαυτο
G	εαυτου	εαυτης	εαυτου
D	εαυτω	εαυτη	εαυτω
A	εαυτους	εαυτας	εαυτα
G	εαυτων	εαυτων	εαυτων
D	εαυτοις	εαυταις	εαυτοις

Example: ο ανθρωπος ουκ εσθει εαυτον. (The man does not eat himself)

αλλος

Both ετερος and αλλος are translated as 'other'. αλλος is declined like αυτος and it falls in the predicate position: αλλος, -η, -ο

Example: ο αλλος ανθρωπος / ο ανθρωπος ο αλλος. (The other man)

αλληλους

αλληλους is translated as 'one another' and is only found in the plural. The full declination is:

Declination of αλληλους

A	αλληλους
G	αλληλων
D	αλληλοις

Example: διωκομεν αλληλους (we persecute one another).

The Imperfect of ειμι (I was)

Imperfect of ειμι

ημην	I was
ης, ησθα	you were
ην	he/she/it was
ημεν / ημεθα	we were
ητε	you (pl) were
ησαν	they were

Exercises

1. The people itself.
2. His own people.
3. The other people.
4. That people.
5. The whole people.
6. This people.
7. In the beginning was the Word.
8. This is the love of God.
9. The same disciples were giving thanks to the rich tax-collector.
10. You used to see her sons in the house.
11. We ourselves were receiving them into the other boat.
12. You were in the temple in those days.

1. ο λαος αυτος.
2. ο ιδιος λαος.
3. ο αλλος λαος.
4. εκεινος ο λαος.

53

5. ολος ο λαος.

6. ουτος ο λαος.

7. Εν αρχη ην ο λογος.

8. αυτη εστιν η αγαπη του Θεου.

9. οι αυτοι μαθηται ηυχαριστουν τω πλουσιω τελωνη.

10. εβλεπες τους υιους αυτης εν τω οικω.

11. αυτοι παρελαμβανομεν αυτους εις το ετερον πλοιον.

12. ης εν τω ιερω εν εκειναις ταις ημεραις.

Vocabulary

αλλος -η -o	other, another
αλληλους	one another
αυτος -η -o	personal pronoun (he).
ευτον -ην -o	reflexive pronoun (himself)

Time and Prepositions

Time

The sense of time can be represented with three of the cases:

1. Accusative (A): for a length of time.

δυο ημερας: for 2 days

μενουσιν την ημεραν εκειην: they remain for that day

2. Genitive (G): for a kind of time (e.g. during the day / night)

ημερας: by day

3. Dative (D): for a precise place or time.

τη τριη ημερᾳ: on the 3rd day.

Prepositions

The meaning of the Preposition can change with the case. The following table gives the meaning of various prepositions when used with a particular cases.

Prepositions

	Meaning	Example	Translation
δια			

A	because of	δια τουτο	because of this
G	through	δια του ιερου	through the temple
μετα			
A	after	μετα ταυτα	after these things
G	with	μετ' αυτων	with them
υπερ			
A	above	υπερ μαθητην	above a disciple
G	on behalf of	υπερ των μαθητων	on behalf of the disciples
υπο			
A	under	υπο εξουσιν	under authority
G	by (person)	υπο του διαβολου	by the devil
κατα			
A	according to	κατα τον διδασκαλον	according to the teacher
G	against	κατα του λαου	against the people
περι			
A	around		
G	concerning		
παρα			
A	alongside	βαλλει αυτο παρα την οδον	he throws it beside the way.
G	from	ανθρωπος παρα του Θεου	a man from God
D	in the presence of	μενουσιν παρ' αυτω	they remain with him
επι			
A	across, upon	βαλλει αλλα επι	He throws others on

		τον πετρον	the rock.
G	upon, in the time of ,on	επ' 'Ηρωδης	In the time of Harod
D	on, against, at		

Additional Note

While in English 'there' and 'it' are explicitly used in a preparatory sense, in Greek they are omitted.

Example: εστιν οινος εν τω οικω : There is wine in the house.

Exercises

1. They were departing privately to their own houses.
2. God was leading them through temptation until the last day.
3. God is for his people, but the workmen of Satan are against the church.
4. The evil man is dead because of sin.
5. After this we used to speak to one another.
6. They know about clothes apart from the teaching of the book.

1. υπηγον κατ' ιδιαν εις τας ιδιας οικας.
2. ο Θεος ηγεν αυτους δια περασμου εως της εσχατης ημερας.
3. ο Θεος εστιν υπερ του λαου αυτου, αλλ' οι εργαται του Σατανα εισιν κατα της εκκλησιας.
4. ο πονηρος εστιν νεκρος δια την αμαρτιαν.
5. μετα τουτο ελαλουμεν αλληλοις.
6. γινωσκουσιν περι ιματια χωρις απο της διδαχης του βιβλιου.

Vocabulary

κατα	against, down upon (gen) - according to (acc)
παρα	from (gen) - near, presence of (dat), alongside (acc)
επι	upon, in the time of, on (gen) - on,against, at (dat), across, upon (acc)
περι	concerning (gen) - around (acc)
προ	before (gen)
συν	with (dat)
δια	because, on account of (acc) - through (gen)
απο	from (gen)
εις	into,unto, against (acc)
εκ	out of (gen)
εν	in,among (dat)
μετα	with (gen) - after (acc)
προς	to,toward (acc)
υπερ	on behalf of (gen) - above,over(acc)
υπο	by means of (gen), under(acc)
προ	before (of place or time)
ενωπιον	before (place)
εμπροσθεν	before (place)
οπισω	after (place)
εξω	outside, out of
χωρις	apart from
αχρι	until, as far as
εως	until, as far as

Note: The last 8 words take the genitive.

The Passive Voice

The passive voice in Greek is formed as follows for the present indicative:

Passive present indicative

λυομαι	I am being loosed
λυῃ	you are being loosed
λυεται	he/she/it are being loosed
λυομεθα	we are being loosed
λυεσθε	you (pl.) are being loosed
λυονται	they are being loosed

And for the imperfect:

Imperfect present indicative

ελυομην	I was being loosed
ελυου	you were being loosed
ελυετο	he/she/it was being loosed
ελυομεθα	we were being loosed
ελυεσθε	you (pl) were being loosed
ελυοντο	they were being loosed

In the case of -εω verbs, the usual contractions take place:

φιλεομαι → φιλουμαι

φιλεη → φιλη

φιλεεται → φιλειται

φιλεομεθα → φιλουμεθα

φιλεετε → φιλειτε

φιλεονται → φιλουνται

similarly for the imperfect:

εφιλεομην → εφιλουμην

εφιλεου → ωφιλου

εφιλεετο → εφιλειτο

εφιλεομεθα → εφιλουμεθα

εφιλεεσθε → εφιλεισθε

εφιλεοντο → εφιλουντο

The passive is often accompanied by what is known as an agent (person) or instrument. The agent is often introduced by the preposition υπο (by) while an instrument is simply in the dative case. An example of both forms used in the same sentence would be:

ο ανθρωπος πεμπεται υπο του αποστολου λογω : the man is being sent by the apostle with a word

Exercises

1. The word of God was being read by the apostles.
2. The tomb was being built under the temple.
3. Because of this the judges were being persuaded by the faithful teachers.
4. You were leading the people after the beloved prophet through the desert to Jerusalem.
5. After this they were being sought for by the whole crowd.
6. The stones were upon the earth above the river.

1. Ο λογος του Θεου ανεγινωσκετο υπο τους αποστολους.
2. το μνημειον ωκοδομειτο υπο το ιερον.
3. δαι τουτο οι κριναι επειθοντο υπο των πιστων διδασκαλων.
4. ηγες τον λαον οπισω του αγαπητου προφητου δια της ερηνου εις τα Ιεροσολυμα.
5. μετα τουτο εζητουντο υπο ολου του οχλου.
6. οι λιθος ησαν επι τω γω υπερ τον ποταμον.

The Relative Pronoun and Present Imperative

The Relative Pronoun

The endings for εκεινος and αυτος form the relative pronoun (who, that, whom, whose):

Relative Pronouns

		M	F	N
Singular	N	ὁς	ἥ	ὅ
	A	ον	ην	ὅ
	G	ου	ης	ου
	D	ῳ	ῃ	ῳ
Plural	N	οι	αι	α
	A	οι	ας	α
	G	ων	ων	ων
	D	οις	αις	οις

Generally rough breathing marks would appear on these pronouns (as shown on the first line). Because these pronouns refer back to a noun the are called the noun's antecedent. However, as mentioned earlier, we are leaving off accents to make it easier to learn.

Example: θεωρω τους αποστολους οι ακολουθουσιν : I see the apostles who are following.

Although αποστολος is in the accusative (A) case, its antecedent is in the nominative (N) case since it functions as such in its clause.

The Present Imperative

The imperative mood is used for commands. In the present active tense it is a linear action, so it expresses the need to continue doing an action or to do it repeatedly.

Imperative of λυω

	Active		Passive	
Singular	λυε	loose	λυου	be loosed
	λυετω	let him loose	λυεσθω	let him be loosed
Plural	λυετε	loose	λυεσθε	be loosed
	λυετωσαν	let them loose	λυεσθωσαν	let them be loosed

for -εω verbs the usual contractions take place:

Contractions

Active	Passive
φιλεε → φιλει	φιλου
φιλεετω → φιλειτω	φιλεισθω
φιλεετε → φιλειτε	φιλεισθε
φιλεετωσαν → φιλειτωσαν	φιλεισθωσαν

The following are over-translations to demonstrate the meaning.

Examples:

- μη εκβαλλετε τα διαμονια: do not continue casting out demons
- πεμπετω τα δορα : let him continue to send gifts.

As the first example shows, imperatives are negated with μη rather than ου.

Exercises

1. Therefore let it be thrown beside the way.
2. Be loosed from sin daily.
3. Be saved from the authority of evil men.
4. Let the commandments themselves be kept.
5. Let him be led away to the council of Caiaphas.
6. Let not the clean dwell in the midst of sin, nor unclean hearts have joy in the rewards of the rich.
7. There was a beautiful boat upon the sea, but the people did not have money for it.
8. Let the teacher who is worthy of honor believe the book and worship God.

1. διο βαλλετω παρα την οδον.
2. λυου απο της αμαρτιας κατ' ημερα.
3. σωζεσθε απο της εξουσιας πονηρων.
4. αι εντολαι αυται τηρεισθεσαν.
5. απαγεσθω εις το συνηδριον του Καιαφα.
6. οι καθαροι μη κατοικειτωσαν εν μεσω της αμαρτιας, μηδε αι ακαθαραι καρδιαι εχετωσαν χαραν εν τοις μισθοις των πλουσιων.
7. ην καλον πλοισον επι τη θαλασση, αλλ' ο λαος ουκ ειχεν αργυριον αυτω.

8. ο διδασκαλος ος εστιν αχιους της τιμης πιστευεσθω τω βιβλιω και προσκυνειτω τω Θεω.

Personal, Possessive and Reflexive Pronouns

Personal Pronouns

The pronouns for the 1st and 2nd person are:

Pronouns

Singular	N	εγω	συ
	A	εμε,με	σε
	G	εμου, μου	σου
	D	εμοι, μοι	σοι
Plural	N	ημεις	υμεις
	A	ημας	υμας
	G	ημων	υηων
	D	ημιν	υμιν

the longer, εμε, εμου and εμοι suggest emphasis.

Since in Greek the verb contains the pronoun, the nominative pronoun in 'εγω λυω' is unnecessary, but rather instead suggests an emphasis on the pronoun. e.g. ουκ ως εγω θελω, αλλ' ως συ : not as **I** will but as **you** [will].

For the third person pronoun, the following forms may be used. Here they are ranked from most common to least:

1. αυτος
2. ουτος, εκιενος

66

3. an article followed by δε.

Examples:

- ουτος ἡν ἐν αρχη : he was in the beginning.
- εκεινοι λευγουσιν αυτη : they say to her.
- ο δε λεγει αυτοις : he says to them.

μεν ... δε

The form, 'μεν ... δε', can either mean: 1) some ... others or 2) on one hand ... on the other.

Examples:

- Εγω μεν ειμι Παυλου, Εγω δε Απολλω : I am of Paul, and I of Apollos.
- οι μεν ησαν συν τοις Ιουδαιοις, οι δε συν τοις αποστολος : Some were with the Jews and others with the apostles.

Possessive

The possessive can be expressed with the pronouns such as μου, συ or αυτου which we have seen before. However it can also be expressed with possessive adjectives, my and your: εμος -η -ov and σος -η -ov.

Examples:

- παρακαλεω σε περι του εμου τεκνον : I beseech you concerning my child.

- η εμη διδαχη ουκ εστιν εμη : My teaching is not mine.

Reflexive Pronouns

Reflexives such as 'myself' or 'yourself' are expressed by combining εμε/σε with αυτος:

Myself:

εμαυτον -ην

εμαυτου -ης

εμαυτῳ -ῃ

Yourself:

σεαυτον -ην

σεαυτου -ης

σεαυτῳ -ῃ

For the plural (ourselves, yourselves, themselves) εαυτους is used.

Examples:

εγω απ' εμαυτου λαλω : I speak from myself.

συ περι σεαυτου μαρτυρεις : You bear witness about yourself.

μαρτυρειτε εαυτοις : You bear witness to yourselves.

Exercises

1. We were calling and weeping, but you used not to have mercy upon us.
2. Some persuade and some exhort only.
3. It used to seem wise to me, but they followed a different way.
4. Lord, have mercy on me daily until your second coming.
5. They take hold of Jesus and injure him.
6. But he used to say "Hypocrite, depart from me."
7. And this is the sign of your second coming.
8. Prayer is being made by me and by your people.
9. You love your enemy as yourself.

1. ημεις μεν εφωνουμεν και εκλαιομεν, υμεις δε ουκ ηλεειτε ημας.
2. οι μεν πειθουσιν και οι δε παρακαλουσιν μονον.
3. εμοι μεν εδομει σοφον, οι δε ηκολουθουν ετερά οδῳ.
4. Κυριος, ελεει με καθ' ημεραν εως σου της δευτερας παρουσιας.
5. οι κρατουσιν τον Ιησουν και αδικουσιν αυτον.
6. ο δε ελεγεν, Υποκριτα, υποαγε απο μου.
7. τουτο δε εστιν το μνημιον της σου δευτερης παρουσιας.
8. προσευχη ποιεται υπο μου και του λαου σου.
9. φιλει τον σον εχθρον ως σεαυτον.

Vocabulary

ως	as
καθως	as, even as
ωσπερ	just as, even as
μεν	not
εγω	I

καγω	and I
κακεινος	and that
συ	you
ημεις	we
υμεις	you
εμος	my
σος	yours
εμαυτον	myself
σεαυτον	yourself

δυναμαι and the Infinitive

δυναμαι

δυναμαι (to be able) has the following conjugation in the indicative:

δυναμαι

Present	Imperfect
δυναμαι	εδυναμην
δυνασαι	εδυνασο
δυναται	εδυνατο
δυναμεθα	εδυναμεθα
δυνασθε	εδυνασθε
δυνανται	εδυναντο

Infinitive: δυνασθαι.

Infinitive

For ειμι, φιλεω and λυω the infinitives are as follows:

Active:

λυειν (to loose)

φιλειν (to love)

ειναι (to be)

Passive:

λυεσθαι (to be loosed)

φιλεισθαι (to be loved)

The infinitive may function as a noun (subject or object) or a verb. When the infinitive (inf.) acts as a verb its "subject" is in the accusative (A) case.

Note:

- εξεστιν (it is lawful) and παραγγελλω (I command) are exceptions in that they take the dative case.
- μη is used to negate infinitives.
- ωστε (so that) is used to express the result of the main verb.

Examples

- εξεστιν θεραπευειν εν τω σαββατω : It is lawful to heal on the Sabbath. (The inf. is the sub.)
- παραγγελλει τον Παυλον αγεσθαι : He commands Paul to be brought
- δει ανθρωπον εσθιεν : A man must eat.
- ωστε μη χρειν εχειν ημας : so that we have no need.

The Articular Infinitive

Articles are often combined with prepositions with the following meanings:

εν + dative = while

προ + genitive = before

μετα + accusative = after

δια + accusative = because

The articles may come from regular nouns, or they may come from infinitives, which are acting as nouns.

Examples:

- εν δε τω υπαγειν αυτον οι οχλοι συνεπνιγον αυτον : while he was departing, the crowds crowded him.
- ειχον προ του τον κοσμον ειναι παρα σοι : [The glory] I had with you before the world was.
- μετα το παραδοθαναι τον Ιωανην : After John was arrested.
- δια το ειναι φιλον : because he was a friend.

Note: To express a purpose the infinitive can be used 1) alone, 2) with εις or προς + accusative, 3) with του.

Examples:

- εζητουν κατα του Ιησου μαρτυριαν εις το θανατωσαι αυτον : they were seeking a witness against Jesus, in order to have him killed.

- εις το δυνασθαι ημας παρακαλειν : in order that we may be able to encourage.
- προς το δυασθαι υμας : in order that you may be able
- υπαγω αλιευειν : I am departing to fish.
- μελλει γαρ Ηρωδης ζητειν το παιδιον του απολεσαι αυτο : For Herod is about to seek the child to destroy it.

Exercises

1. For you have need of us to teach you the truth.
2. But are bad men able to find wisdom?
3. Did he not wish to be released from sin?
4. They were not willing to obey the elders.
5. I am a man, but you are children.
6. Is it not lawful for them to take money from the tax-collectors?
7. We are sending the slaves to call the blind and poor.
8. We wish to look at the temple of the God of Israel.
9. It was necessary for Jesus to lead the disciples away from Galilee.
10. Jesus is about to ask them to send sufficient bread.

1. χρειαν γαρ εχετε του ημας διδασκειν υμας την αληθειαν.
2. κακοι δε δυνανται ευρισκειν την σοφιαν;
3. ουκ ηθελεν αυτον απολυεσθαι απο της αραρτιας.
4. ουκ ηθελον υπακουιεν τοις πρεσβυτεροις.
5. εγω μεν ειμι ανθρωπος, υμεις δε εστε τεκνα.
6. μη εξεστιν αυτοις λαμβανειν τον αργυριον απο των τελωνων;
7. ημεις πεμπομεν τους δουλους καλειν τους τυφλους και τους πχωτους.
8. θελομεν θεωρειν εις το ιερον του Θεου Ισραηλ.
9. εδει τον Ιησουν απαγειν τους μαθητας απο της Γαλιλαιας.
10. ο Ιησους μελλει αιτειν αυτους πεμπειν ικανον αρτον.

Vocabulary

δυναμαι	I am able.
θελω	I will, wish
μελλω	I am about
δει	it is necessary
εξεστι	it is lawful
ωστε	with the result that, so that

The Future Tense

The future active tense (I will/shall loose) has the same conjugation as the present but the letter σ is present after the stem:

λυσω

λυσεις

λυσει

λυσομεν

λυσετε

λυσουσι(ν)

When the stem ends with one of following letters, contractions occur:

κ, γ, χ + σ → ξ

π, β, φ + σ → ψ

τ, δ, θ + σ → σ

for -εω verbs ε changes to its lengthened form η, although καλεω is an exception.

Verb Contraction Examples

ανοιγω →-ανοιξω

εχω → εξω

βλεπω → βλεψω

γραφω → γραψω

πειθω → πεισω

καλεω → καλεσω (exception)

φιλεω → φιλησω

Exercises

1. And you have the authority to walk in Galilee.
2. I will open the books which are in the synagogue.
3. We will behold the face of the Lord in the temple which is being built in Jerusalem.
4. We will send slaves to pursue them as far as Judea.
5. He will speak these things to the crowd in parables.
6. Do not bless evil men, for evil men will not see the sun.

1. και εχεις τον εξουσια του περιματειν εν τη Γαλιλαια.
2. ανιοξω τα βιβλια ά εστιν εν τη συνηγαγη.
3. θεωρησομεν το προσωπον του Κυριου εν τω ιερω ὅ οικοδομειται εν τοις Ιεροσολεμοις.
4. πεμψομεν δουλους διωκειν αυτους εως της Ιουδαιας.
5. λαλησει ταυτα τοις οχλοις εν παραβολαις.

6. ουκ ευλογει πονηρους, οι γαρ πονηροι ου βλεψουσιν τον ηλιον.

The Stem of a Verb

Up to this point we have only dealt with the present stem, which is used in the present and imperfect tenses. However the more important stem is the verbal stem, from which the present stem is usually derived. It is also the principle stem for the other tenses, many of which we have not encountered yet. Some examples of verb classes where the verbal and present stem differ are:

1. Verbs that add a τ to the verbal stem to form the present tense:

τ endings

Verbal Stem	Present	Future	Translation
αποκαλυπ	αποκαλυπτω	αποκαλυψω	I reveal
κρυπ	κρυπτω	κρυψω	I hide

2. Verbs with guttural endings that soften the present tense with σσ:

σσ endings

κηρυκ	κηρυσσω	κηρυξω	I preach / proclaim
πραγ	πρασσω	πραξω	I do

3. Verbs that have a -ζω ending in the present:

ζω endings

79

| βαπτιδ | βαπτιζω | βαπτισω | I baptize |
| δοξαδ | δοξαζω | δοξασω | I glorify |

Exercises

1. The faithful widow will sit alone in prayer and her witness will not cause the other women to stumble.
2. He will have mercy upon me, and I shall have eternal salvation.
3. Buy your sacrifices and sanctify the Sabbath.
4. The disciples whom John was baptizing remained with Jesus
5. Will he not reveal his face to the unbelieving soul?

1. η πιστη χηρα καθισει μονος εν προσευχη και η αυτης μαρτυρια ου σκανδαλισει τας αλλας.
2. ελεησει με, και εξω αιωιον σωτηριαν.
3. αγοραζετε τας Θυσιας υμων και αγιαζετε το σαββατον.
4. οι μαθηται ους ο Ιωανης εβαπτιζεν εμενον μετα του Ιησου
5. ουκ αποκαλυψει το προσωπον τη απιστη ψυχη;

Vocabulary

απο-καλυπτω	I reveal
κρυπτω	I hide
βαπτιζω	I baptize
εγγιζω	I draw near
ελπιζω	I hope
καθαριζω	I cleanse
καθιζω	I seat, sit
ακανδαλιζω	I cause to stumble
αγιαζω	I sanctify
αγοραζω	I buy

βασταζω	I carry
δοξαζω	I glorify
ετοιμαζω	I prepare
θαυμαζω	I wonder at
πειραζω	I test, tempt
κραζω	I cry out
κηρυσσω	I proclaim
πρασσω	I do
φυλασσω	I guard

The Middle Voice and The future of ειμι

The Middle Voice

The middle form of a verb sits somewhere in meaning between the active and passive voices, although generally it is closer to the active in meaning. For example λυομαι would be could be translated as either, (1) I loose for myself (middle) **or** (2) I am being loosed (passive).

In the case of the verb ενδω (I put clothes on) we would have two possible renderings:

1. ενδω X Y: I put X on Y (active)
2. ενδυομαι X : I put X on myself. (middle)

A Deponent verb: This is a verb that is middle in form but active in meaning. There are many examples of these in the vocabulary list.

Note: A verb may change voices depending on the tense. For example:

γινωσκω : I know (active)

γωνσκομαι : I will know (middle)

Sometimes the meaning of the verb will change drastically between the active and middle form. For example:

αρχω : I rule

αρχομαι : I begin

The conjugation of the middle voice for λυω is:

The middle voice of λυω

Present:	λυομαι	Imperfect:	ελυομην
	λυῃ		
	λυεται	Imperative:	λυου
	λυομεθα		
	λυεσθε	Infinitive:	λυεσθαι
	λυονται		

which is the same as the passive.

The future middle is the same as the present tense but with a 'σ' located between the stem and the endings:

The Future Middle

λυσομαι

λυσῃ

λυσεται

λυσομεθα

λυσεσθε

λυσονται

The future of ειμι is uses εσ- as a stem, and it has only one irregularity in the 3rd person singular.

The Future of ειμι

εσομαι

εση

εσται

εσομεθα

εσεσθε

εσονται

Exercises

1. Reckon yourselves to be dead.
2. Shall I become a power friend like the rich man?
3. The evil ruler feared John.

4. The church becomes like a beautiful virgin, who God is preparing for eternal life.
5. And you shall be holy to the Lord.
6. Therefore we shall take the cup of salvation with joy.
7. And I shall know as he knows.
8. We wished to go and greet you, but he wishes you to come and pray with us.
9. But I will become wise and will come to him in the fear of the Lord.
10. He will not injure his own right eye, will he?

1. λογιζετε σεαυτους αναθαντατειν
2. γενησομαι δυνατος φιλος ομοιος πλοσιω ανθροπω;
3. ο πονηρος αρχων εφοβειτο Ιωανην.
4. η εκκλησια γινεται ομοις καλη παρθενω, ην ο Θεος ετοιμαζει εις ζωνη αιωνιον.
5. εσεσθε δε αγιοι τω Κυριω.
6. λημβομεθα ουν το ποτηριον της σωτηριας μετα χαρας.
7. καγω γνωσομαι ως αυτος γινωσκει.
8. εβουλομεθα πορευχεσθαι και ασπαζεσθαι υμας, ο δε βουλεται υμας ερχεσθαι και προσευχεσθαι μεθ' υμας.
9. γενησομαι δε σοφος και ελευσομαι προς αυτον εν τω φοβω του Κυριου.
10. μη αδικησει τον ιδιον δεξιον οφθαλμον;

Vocabulary

αρχω	I rule
αρχομαι	I begin
υπαρχω	I am, exist
απτομαι	I take hold of, touch
αρνεομαι	I deny

ασπαζομαι	I greet
δεχομαι	I receive, welcome
εργαζομαι	I work
ερχομαι	I come, go
ελευσομαι	I will come, go
απερχομαι	I go away
διερχομαι	I go through
εισερχομαι	I go into, come into
εξερχομαι	I go out
προσερχομαι	I come to
συνερχομαι	I come together
ευαγγελιζομαι	I bring good news
προσευχομαι	I pray
βουλομαι	I will, wish
φοβεομαι	I fear
αποκρινομαι	I answer
γινομαι	I become
γενησομαι	I will become
παραγινομαι	I am beside, I come.
πορευομαι	I go
εκπορευομαι	I go out.
λογιζομαι	I reckon

The First Aorist

The aorist is a point tense referring to specific event in time rather than a continuous or repeated action like the present or imperfect. There are two different forms: first (or weak) and second (or strong). Usually a verb has either one or the other.

The aorist conjugation of λυω is,

Indicative		Imperative	
ελυσα	I loosed	λυσον	loose
ελυσας	you loosed	λυσατω	let him loose
ελυσε(ν)	he/she/it loosed	λυσατε	loose (pl)
ελυσαμεν	we loosed	λυσατωσαν	let them loose
ελυσατε	you (pl.) loosed	**Infinitive**	
ελυσαν	they loosed	λυσαι	to loose

Note: Only the indicative has the augment (ε) since the imperative and infinitive do not refer to the past. This same augment is used for the imperfect tense.

Note: The first aorist is characterized by 'σα' after the stem. Like the future tense, this may cause changes to the stem.

Present	Future	First Aorist
κραζω	κραξω	εκραξα

κηρυσσω	κηρυξω	εκηρυξα
φιλεω	φιλησω	εφιλησα
καλεω	καλεσω	εκαλεσα
θελω	θελησς	ηθελησα

Note: The last two rows have irregular conjugations

The Aorist Infinitive

The aorist infinitive differs from the present infinite in that it refers to a point in time rather than something continuous.

For example:

γραφειν καλον εστιν υμιν : To continue writing is good for you.

ελπιζω γραψαι επιστολην : I hope to write you a letter.

Exercises

1. And they baptized the tax-collectors in the river.
2. You were going through the beautiful land to prepare the free people.
3. Strong workman, hide the stones which abound in the field.
4. Do not continue to cause the brethren who were ill to stumble.
5. But they followed one another.

6. For you revealed the commandments and promises to the church.
7. Shall we begin to read the books?
8. Cleanse and sanctify your hearts.
9. Is it lawful for them to heal on the Sabbath?

1. εβαπτισαν δε τους τελωνας εν τω ποταμω.
2. διηρχεσθε την καλην γην ετοιμασαι τον ελευθερον λαον.
3. εργατα ισχυρε κρυψον τους λιθους ὅι περισσυουσιν εν τω αργω.
4. μη σκανδαλιζετε τους αδελπους ὅι ησθενουν.
5. ηκολουθησαν δε αλληλοις.
6. απεκαλυψατε γαρ τας εντολας και τας επαγγελιας τη εκκλησια.
7. αρξομεθα αναγινωσκειν τα βιβλια;
8. καθαρισατε και αγγιασατε τας καρδιας υμων.
9. εξεστιν αυτοις θεραπευειν εν τω σαββατω;

The Second Aorist

The Second Aorist has the same meaning as the first, but its endings follow the pattern of the imperfect. Generally it is characterized by a change in the stem. For example the verb βαλλω (I throw) has the second Aorist form:

Indicative	Imperative
εβαλον	βαλε
εβαλες	βαλετω
εβαλε(ν)	βαλετε
εβαλομεν	βαλετωσαν
εβαλομεθα	**Infinitive**
εβαλον	βαλειν

Some other common second aorist verbs are listed below:

Present	Second Aorist	English
αγω	ηγαγον	I lead

αμαρτανω	ημαρτον	I sin
αποθνησκω	απεθανον	I die
βαλλω	εβαλον	I throw
ευρισκω	ευρον	I find
εχω	εσχον	I have
καταλειπω	κατελιπον	I leave
λαμβανω	ελαβον	I take
μανθανω	εμαθον	I learn
πασχω	επαθον	I suffer
πινω	επιον	I drink
πιπτω	επεσον	I fall
φευγω	εφυγον	I flee
ερχομαι	ηλθον*	I go/come
εσθιω	εφαγον	I eat

λεγω	ειπον*	I say
οραω	ειδον*	I see
φερω	ηνεγκον*	I carry

* these verbs often have First Aorist ending added to the second aorist stem, e.g. ελθατω η βασιλεια σου (Your kingdom come).

The verb γινωσκω and the compound verbs which have the stem –βαινω (I go) have irregular Second Aorist forms:

εγνων	-εβην
εγνωνς	-εβης
εγνω	-εβη
εγνωμεν	-εβημεν
εγνωτε	-εβητε
εγνωσαν	-εβησαν

Exercises

1. Therefore we cast ourselves into the river.

2. But you took the clothes which the elders sent for the poor.
3. Did they then flee from the face of the judges?
4. This is the stone that fell from heaven.
5. The virgin had a son, and they called him Jesus.
6. For the Son of man must suffer.
7. After these days we went to Galilee.

1. εβαλομεν ουν εμαυτους εις τον ποταμον.
2. ελαβες δε τα ιματια ἁ οι πρεσβυτεροι επεμψον τοις πτωχοις.
3. εφυγον αρα απο του προσωπου των κριτων;
4. ουτος εστιν ο λιθος ὁς επεσεν εκ του ουρανου.
5. η παρθενος εσχεν υιον και εκαλεσαν αυτον Ιησουν.
6. δει γαρ τον υιον του ανθρωπου παθειν.
7. μετα ταυτα τας ημερας ελθομεν εις την Γαλιλαιαν.

The Future and Aorist of liquid Verbs and the word οτι

Liquid Verbs

Stems which end with a λ,μ,ν or ρ (the word 'lemoners' may help to remember these) are known as liquid verbs. These verbs do not have a 'σ' between the stem and ending, and their future endings follow the pattern of the φιλεω. Since the endings are the same for many of the verb forms accents must be used to demonstrate the intended tense, e.g.

Present: κρινω, κρινεις, κρινει, κρινομεν, κρινετε, κρινουσιν

Future: κρινῶ, κρινεῖς, κρινεῖ, κρινουμεν, κρινειτε, κρινοῦσιν

Common liquid verb examples

Present	Future	Aorist	Translation
αιρω	αρω	ηρα	I lift up
σπειρω	σπερω	εσπειρα	I sow
εγειρω	εγερω	ηγειρα	I raise
αποκτεινω	αποκτενω	απεκτινα	I kill
αποστελλω	αποστελλω	απεστειλα	I send

αγγελλω	αγγελω	ηγγειλα	I announce
μενω	μενῶ	εμεινα	I remain
κρινω	κρινῶ	εκρινα	I judge
βαλλω	βαλω	εβαλον	I throw

The Word οτι

οτι is often best translated by the English words "that" or "because".

Examples:

θεωρω οτα προφητης εστιν αυτος : I see that he is a prophet.

υμεις λεγει οτι Βλασφημεις, οτι ειπον Υιος του Θεου ειμι (John 10:36) : You say, "You are blaspheming", because I said, "I am the Son of God".

The last example shows how οτι can introduce a direct statement, which does not require it to be directly translated.

When it comes to statements about the past, Greek differs from English. In English we would say: 'When I *spoke* with Sarah yesterday, I heard you *were* away.' The initial clause is set in the past, since I spoke with Sarah yesterday. While in Engilsh, the

95

second clause is also set in the past, in Greek the second clause is set in the present since at the time I spoke with Sarah she would have told me that, 'you are away'. This means that,*when translating from Greek to English the dependent statement should be translated one tense further into the past.* Take note of this when doing the exercises.

Exercises

1. Send the young men to rouse the soldiers.
2. But he took the child and departed.
3. They will not die in the desert, for the soldiers will save them.
4. Therefore I judge my people at that time.
5. And the Pharisees went to eat bread with the prophet.
6. And when he heard these words he sent them to kill his enemy.
7. They will remain in the house while the paralyzed man is dying.
8. We announced therefore that the apostle had fallen.

1. αποστειλον τους νεανιας εγειραι τους στρατιωτας.
2. ελαβεν δε το παιδον και υπηγεν.
3. ουκ αποθανουσιν εν τη ερημῶ, οι γαρ στρατιωται σωσυοσιν αυτους.
4. κρινῶ ουν τον λαον μου εν εκεινῳ τῳ καιρῳ.
5. οι δε Παρισαιαι ηλθον φαγειν αρτον παρα τῶ προφητη.
6. και οτε ηκουσεν τουτους τους λογους απεστειλεν αυτους αποκτειναι τον εχθρον αυτου.
7. μενοῦσιν εν τῶ οικῶ εως ο παραλυτικος αποθνησκει.
8. απεστειλαμεν ουν οτι ο αποστολος επασεν.

Vocabulary

οφειλω	I owe
οτε	when
εως	while *or* until

The First and Second Aorist Middle

The middle for first and second aorists follows the pattern of the imperfect middle. For λυω (I loose) and γινομαι(I become) this is given below:

First Aorist		Second Aorist	
Indicative	**Imperative**	**Indicative**	**Imperative**
ελυσαμην	λυσαι	εγενομην	γενου
ελυσω	λυσασθω	εγενου	γενεσθω
ελυσατο	λυσασθε	εγενατο	γενεσθε
ελυσαμεθα	λυσασθωσαν	εγενομεθα	γενεσθωσαν
ελυσασθε	**Infinitive**	εγενεσθε	**Infinitive**
ελυσαντο	λυσασθαι	εγενοντο	γενεσθαι

Notice that the first aorist inserts its characteristic σα, while the second aorist has the change of stem and omits the σα.

Mostly the middle is used for deponent verbs. The standard rules for combining augments and endings apply. Some examples are given below:

Present	Aorist
απτομαι	ηψαμην
αρχομαι	ηρξαημν
δεχομαι	εδεξαμην
εργαζομαι	ηργασαμην

| ευαγγελιζομαι | ευηγγελισαμην |

γινομαι is one of the more commonly used verbs in the middle. It is often used for the imperative instead of ειμι, e.g. μη γινεσθε ως οι υποκριται (do not be as the hypocrites- Matt 6:16). It is also commonly used in the expression, 'it came to be'. E.g.

εγενετο φωνη εκ της νεφελης (Mark 9:7): There came to be a voice out of the clouds.

και εγενετο και αυτος διηρχετο (Luke 17:11): and it came to be and he went through.

Exercises

1. And Jesus began to say to the crowds concerning John, 'He prepared my way'.
2. Let a man deny himself and come after me.
3. Peter, go into the house of the unbelieving woman and greet her.
4. And on that day the remaining saints preached the gospel and worked righteousness.
5. But he went up into the temple to pray.
6. Sinner, receive the word with fear.

1. ηρξατο δε ο Ιησους λεγειν τοις οχλοις περι Ιωανου οτι Ητοιμασεν την οδον μου.
2. ανθρωπος αργησασθω εαυτον και ελθετω οπισω μου.
3. Πετρε ελθε εις την οικιαν της απιστου και ασπασαι αυτην.
4. εν δε εκεινη ημερα οι λοιποι αγιοι ευηγγελισαντο και ηργασαντο δικαιοσυνην.

5. ανεβη δε εις το ειρον προσευξασθαι.
6. αμαρτωλε, δεξαι τον λογον μετα φοβου.

The 3rd Declension

This class of nouns incompasses all nouns which do not fall within the 1st and 2nd declension. In this lesson we examine masculine and feminine nouns whose stems end with a consonant.

In general, third declension nouns have a set pattern for all the cases with the exception of the singular nominative case. As a result, in lexicons both the nominative and genitive are given along with the article which denotes the gender. So for example one would fine 'ελπις, ελπιδος, η' under the entry for 'hope'.

The endings are as follows:

Third Declension Endings

	Singular	Plural
N	variable	ες
A	α	ας
G	ος	ων
D	ι	σι(ν)

Note: The vocative is generally the same as the nominative, so it is left out of the tables.

As an example we give the declension of the word 'star', which has the lexicon entry, 'αστηρ, αστερος, ο':

αστηρ	αστηρες
αστηρα	αστηρας
αστηρος	αστηρων
αστηρι	αστηρσι(v)

Since the plural dative starts with a 'σ', changes in the stem may occur. The following rules often apply, although there are exceptions:

κ,γ,χ + σιν → ξιν

π,β,φ + σιν → ψιν

τ,δ,θ,v + σιν → σιν

αντ + σιν → ασιν

εντ + σιν → εισιν

οντ + σιν → ουσιν

Examples Of the Dative Plural

English	N	G	D (pl.)
age	αιων	αιωνος	αιωσιν
night	νυξ	νυκτος	νυξιν
flesh	σαρξ	σαρκος	σαρξιν
ruler	αρχων	αρχοντος	αρχουσιν

Certain nouns have irregular forms such as πατηρ (father), ματηρ (mother) and θυγατηρ (daughter). These all have the same general declension as πατηρ, which is given below. Pay close attention to the bolded entries.

πατηρ	πατερες
πατερα	πατερας
πατρος	πατερων
πατρι	**πατρασι(ν)**

Exercises

1. Woman, you did not find sufficient money for the rulers, did you?
2. And the teacher himself sent his own children into the vineyard.
3. But the night and the day will not remain for ever and ever.
4. After these things we looked at the star with them.
5. And we announced that he was a Savior for women.

6. Their flesh is weak, but the witnesses are being saved by grace.
7. But they worked with the hands and the feet.

1. γυναι, ουκ ευρες ικανον αργυριον τοις αρχουσιν;
2. ο δε διδασκαλος ουτος επεμψεν τους ιδιος παιδας εις τον αμπελωνα.
3. αλλ'η νυξ και η ημερα ου μενοῦσιν εις τους αιωνας των αιωνων.
4. μετα ταυτα εθεωρησαμεν εις τον αστερα μετ' αυτων.
5. απηγγειλαμεν δε οτι εστιν σωτηρ γυναιξιν.
6. η σαρξ αυτων ασθενει, αλλ' οι μαρτυρες σωζονται τη χαριτι.
7. ηργασαντο δε ταις χερσιν και τοις ποσιν.

Vocabulary

ανηρ ανδρος ο	man, husband
αστηρ αστερος ο	star
μαρτυς μαρτυρος ο	witness
σωτηρ σωτηρος ο	savior
χειρ χειρος η	hand
γυνη γυναικος η	woman
σαρξ σαρκος η	flesh
ελπις ελπιδος η	hope

νυξ νυκτος η	night
παις παιδος ο/η	boy, girl,child,servant
πους ποδος ο	foot
χαρις χαριτος η	grace
αιων αιωνος ο	age
εις τον αιωνα	forever
αμπελων αμπελωνος ο	vineyard
εικων εικονος η	image
Ελλην Ελληνος ο	Greek
μην μηνος ο	month
Σιμων Σιμωνος ο	Simon
αρχων αρχοντος ο	ruler
θυγατηρ η	daughter
μητηρ η	mother

πατηρ ο	father

Irregularities:

father (voc.) πατερ

grace (acc. sing.) χαριν

woman (voc. sg.) γυναι

man (dat. pl.) ανδρασιν

hands (dat. pl.) χερσιν

Neuter Nouns of the 3rd Declension

Neuter nouns are characterized by two different types.

First Type

The first type have the following endings:

First Type Endings

	Singular	Plural
N.A.	variable	-α
G	-ος	-ων
D	-ι	-σι(ν)

An example is 'σωμα, σωματος, το' (body).

Full Declension of σωμα (body)

N.A.	σωμα	σωματα
G	σωματος	σματων
D	σωματι	σωμασι(ν)

Second Type (-ες endings)

This second type can be difficult to characterize because the -ες endings disappear after contractions take place. Below is an example with the noun 'γενος, γενους, το' (race).

**The Declension of
γενος (race)**

N.A.	γενος	γενη
G	γενους	γενων
D	γενει	γενεσι(ν)

While these endings appear completely different from those of the first type, they are actually the same, but contractions have taken place. They can be formed by taking the root word 'γενες', dropping the σ, and then adding the endings from the first type. E.g. γενε + ος → γενους (G.)

Exercises

1. But God is rich in mercy.
2. He said therefore that he was not the light, but he comes to bear witness about the light.
3. And we went through fire and water, for the spirit of compassion dwelt in us.
4. And he will open the ears of the multitudes who cannot hear.

5. Not even the years of the mountains will be for ever; for the end will be the darkness of the judgment.
6. But we ourselves are members of his body.
7. For the seed of Abraham must eat the Passover.
8. See my hands and my feet.
9. He is the way of light for the multitudes.

1. αλλα ο Θεος εστιν πλουσιος εν ελεει.
2. ειπεν ουν οτι ουκ εστιν το φως, αλλα ερχεται ματυρησαι περι του φωτου.
3. και διηλθομεν δια πυρος και υδατος, το γαρ πνευμα του ελεους κατωκει ημας.
4. ανοιξει δε τα ωτα των πληθων ἁ ου δυναται ακουειν.
5. δεου τα ετη των ορων εσται εις τον αιωνα. το ταρ τελος εσται σκοτος του κριματος.
6. αυτοι δε εσμεν μελον του σωματος.
7. δει γαρ το σπερμα του Αβρααμ φαγειν το πασχα.
8. ιδετε τας χειρας και τους ποδας μου.
9. εστιν η οδος του φωτος τοις πληθεσιν.

Vocabulary

αιμα	blood
βαπτισμα	baptism
θελημα	will
κριμα	judgment
ονομα	name

πνευμα	spirit
ρημα	word
σπερμα	seed
στομα	mouth
σωμα	body
ους ωτος	ear
πυρ πυρος	first
τερας τερατος	a wonder
υδωρ υδατος	water
φως φωτος	light
γενος	race, kind
εθνος	nation
ελεος	mercy
ετος	year

μελος	member
μερος	part
ορος	mountain
πληθος	multitude
σκευος	vessel
σκοτος	darkness
τελος	end
πασχα	Passover
Αβρααμ	Abraham

The words, ους,πυρ,τερας,υδωρ and φως are declined the same as σωμα, but have a different nominative form. The words, γενος,εθνος,ελεος,ετος,μελος,μερος,ορος,πληθος,οκευος,σκοτος and τελος are declined like γενος and the final 2 are indeclinable.

Third Declension adjectives and Interrogative and Indefinite Pronouns

Just as there were two type of neuter nouns in the 3rd declension, so there are two types of adjectives.

Type 1

The adjective πλειων (more) serves as an example of the first type. The endings for the masculine and feminine are the same as nouns of the third declension, while the neuter follows the first type of neuter nouns.

M/F	N	M/F	N
πλειων	πλειον	πλειονες	πλειονα
πλειονα	πλειον	πλειονας	πλειονα
πλειονος	πλειονος	πλειονων	πλειονων
πλειονι	πλειονι	πλειοσιν	πλειοσιν

Only the πλειων, πλειον and πλειονα need to be learned and the rest of the pattern follows the words, αστερ and σωμα.

Type 2

Adjectives with -ες endings are exemplified by the pattern of the adjective αληθης, αληθες (true),

M/F	N	M/F	N
αληθης	αληθες	αληθεις	αληθη
αληθη	αληθες	αληθεις	αληθη
αληθους	αληθους	αληθων	αληθων
αληθει	αληθει	αληθεσι(ν)	αληθεσι(ν)

Interrogative and Indefinite Pronouns

An indefinite pronoun in English is: "someone", "anyone", "a certain person", "a certain thing", etc.

An interrogative pronoun in English is: "who?" or "what?".

In Greek these two types of pronouns differ only by an accent. The interrogative has the accent and it can be augmented with the indefinite relative pronoun (ὁς, ἡ, ὁ), meaning "which" or "who".

The unaccented declension of both pronouns is:

M/F	N	M/F	N
τις	τι	τινες	τινα
τινα	τι	τινας	τινα
τινος	τινος	τινων	τινων
τινι	τινι	τισι(ν)	τισι(ν)

Only τις, τι and τινα need be learned. In the case of the augmented forms (meaning "whoever") both parts decline giving: ὁστις, ἡτις, ὁτι / οἱτινες, αἱτινες, ἁτιωα for the first row (nominative).

Examples

αλλα τί εξηλθατε ιδειν; (Matt 11:8) : But what did you go out to see?

εἰ τις εχει ωτα ακουειν ακουετω (Mark 4:23) : If anyone has ears to hear, let him hear.

τίωα μισθον εχετε; (Matt 5:46) : What reward do you have?

114

γυναικες τινες (Luke 8:2) Certain women

Exercises

1. But they will receive a reward which is better than life.
2. The Christ then is greater than the temple.
3. For he was a man full of grace and truth.
4. The first workmen said, 'We shall receive' more honor'.
5. But the true elders in compassion encourage their weak children.
6. Whoever wishes to come after me, let him deny himself.

1. Παραλημψονται δε τον μισθον ος εστιν κρεισσων ζωης.
2. ο αρα Χριστος εστιν μειζων του ιερου.
3. ην γαρ ανθρωπος πληρης του χαριτος και της αληθειας.
4. οι πρωτοι εργαται ειπον οτι παραλημψομεθα πλειονα τιμην.
5. οι δε αληθεις πρεσβυτεροι εν ελεει παρακαλουσιν τα ασθενη παιδια αυτων.
6. οςτις θελει ελθειν οπισω μου, αρνησασθω εαυτον.

Vocabulary

κρεισσων	better
μειζων	great
πλειων	more
χειρων	worse

αληθης	true
ασθενης	weak,ill,sick
πληρης	full
οστις	whoever
τις	someone

3rd Declension with υ, ι and ευ stems

υ stems

These nouns are relatively uncommon in the New Testament. They follow the pattern of ιχθυς, ιχθους, ὁ (fish) given below. The only difference with regular third declension nouns is in the nominative singular.

A	ιχθυς	ιχθυες
N	**ιχθυν**	ιχθυας
G	ιχθυος	ιχθυων
D	ιχθυϊ	ιχθυσιν

ι stems

Nouns with ι and ευ stems are much more common. The ι stems are all feminine and follow the pattern of πολις, πολεως, η (city)

πολις	πολεις

πολιν	πολεις
πολεως	πολεων
πολει	πολεσι(ν)

εu stems

These nouns are all masculine and follow the pattern of βασιλευς βασιλεως ὁ (king):

βασιλευς	βασιλεις
βασιλεα	βασιλεις
βασιλεως	βασιλεων
βασιλει	**βασιλευσι(ν)**

Note: The εu and ι stemmed nouns have the same ending with the exception of the sigular accusitative and the plural dative which are bolded in the table.

Exercise

1. And the scribes must take the fishes out of the water for the priests.
2. But by his faith he will open the ears of her father.

3. And they marveled that he had been talking with the high-priest.
4. For the men said that they had seen the daughter of the king.
5. In the resurrection whose wife will she be?
6. And my knowledge of the mystery came by (according to) revelation.

1. και δει οι γραμματεις λαβειν τους ιχθυας εκ του ιδατος τοις ιερευσιν.
2. τη δε πιστει αυτου ανοιξει τα ωτας του αυτης πατρος.
3. και εθαυμαζον οτι ελαλει μετα του αρχιερεως.
4. οι γαρ ανδρες ειπον οτι ειδον την θυγατερα του βασιλεως.
5. εν τη αναστασει τινος εσται γυνη;
6. η δε μος γνωσις του μυστηριου ηλθεν κατ' αποκαλυψιν.

Vocabulary

αναστασις	resurrection
αποκαλυψις	revelation
αφεσις	forgiveness
γνωσις	knowledge
δυναμις	power
θλιψις	tribulation, trouble, hardship
κρισις	judgment

παραδοσις	tradition
πιστις	faith
πολις	city
συνειδησις	conscience
γραμματευς	scribe
ιερευς	priest
αρχιερευς	high-priest

Adjectives and pronouns with 1st and 3rd Declensions

The adjective πας (all/every)

πας -σα -ν, follows the 3rd declension for masculine and neuter but the 1st for feminine, as shown below:

πας	πασα	παν	παντες	πασαι	παντα
παντα	πασαν	παν	παντας	πασας	παντα
παντος	πασης	παντος	παντων	πασων	παντων
παντι	παση	παντι	πασι(ν)	πασαις	πασι(ν)

Examples of πας

Standing alone

1. πας ουν οστις ακουει : Therefore everyone who hears
2. παντα διαυτου εγενετο: All things came to be through him.

With a Noun

1. παν δενδρον : Every tree
2. πας ο οχλος : All the crowd

The number 1 (εις)

The number one has the following declension:

M.	F.	N.
εις	μια	εν
ενα	μιαν	εν
ενος	μιας	ενος
ενι	μια̣	ενι

εις can be combined with ου or μη which results in the word 'no one':

ουδεις, ουδεμια,ουδεν // μηδεις, μηδεμια , μηδεν

Examples

πειραζει δε ουδενα

ουκ εφαγεν ουδεν: and he ate nothing (note that the double negative doesn't cancel)

The irregular adjectives: πολυς (much/many) and μεγας(great)

These two irregular adjectives are frequently found in the New Testament.

πολυς	πολλη	πολυ
πολυν	πολλην	πολυ
πολλου	πολλης	πολλου
πολλω	πολλη	πολλω
πολλοι	πολλαι	πολλα

πολλους	πολλας	πολλα
πολλων	πολλων	πολλων
πολλοις	πολλαις	πολλοις

μεγας	μεγαλη	μεγα
μεγαν	μεγαλην	μεγα
μεγαλου	μεταλης	μεταλου
μεταλω	μεταλη	μεταλω
μεγαλοι	μεγαλαι	μεγαλα
μεγαλους	μεγαλας	μεγαλα
μεγαλων	μεγαλων	μεγαλων
μεγαλοις	μεγαλαις	μεγαλοις

Exercises

1. Therefore no one can have two lords.
2. And you will open our mouths, 0 Lord, and every tongue will bless your great name.
3. Did you not sow good seed in the three fields?
4. Do not carry anyone to the synagogue on the Sabbath.
5. But you can heal the colonel.
6. But I came into this world for a great judgment.
7. And one of the lepers, when he saw that he was being healed, threw himself at his feet.
8. For the chief priests knew that this word was true.
9. And all the disciples were full of faith and of the Holy Spirit, and they healed those who were ill (i.e. the ill), and cast out many demons.

1. ουδεις ουν δυναμαι δυο κυριους εχειν.

2. ανοιξεις δε τα στοματα ημων, Κυριε, και πασα γλωσσα ευλογησει το μεγα ονομη σου.
3. ουκ εσπειρας καλον σπερμα εν τοις τρισιναγροις;
4. μη βασταζετε μηδενα εις την συναγωγην εν τω σαββατω.
5. δυνασαι δε θραπευσαι τον χιλιαρχον.
6. ηλθον δε εις τουτον τον κοσμον μεγαλη κρισιν.
7. εις δε εκ των λεπρων, οτε ειδεν οτι θεραπευεται, εβαλεν εαυτον παρα τους ποδας αυτου.
8. οι γαρ αρχειρεις εγνωσαν οτι τουτο το ρημα ην αληθες.
9. και παντες οι μαθηται ησαν πληρεις πιστεως και του αγιου πνευματος, και εθεραπευσαν τους ασθενους, και εξεβαλον πολλα διαμονια.

Vocabulary

πας	all
πολυς	much
μεγας	great
δυο	2
τρεις	3
τεσσαρες –α	4
πεντε	5

εξ	6
επτα	7
δεκα	10
δωδεκα	12
τεσσαρακοντα	40
εκατον	100
χιλιοι –αι –α χιλιας –αδος ἡ	1000
εκατονταρχης	centurion
χιλιαρχος –ου ὁ	captain

Note: the full declension of 3 is:

	M.F.	N.
N.A.	τριες	τρια
G	τριων	τριων
D	τρισι(ν)	τρισι(ν)

and 2 is:

N.A.	δυο
G	δυο
D	δυσιν

Adjectives and Adverbs: Forms for Comparison

Adjectives

A comparative adjective (e.g. more righteous) is formed by replacing the –ος ending with –τερος.

δικαιος δικαιοτερος –α –ον

While a superlative (e.g. most righteous) is formed with the ending, –τατος .

δικαιοτατος –η –ον

If there is a shortened syllable before the ending then the o is lengthened:

σοφος, σοφωτερος, σοφωτατος

The comparative is declined like αγιος since it has a 'ρ' at the end of the stem.

Irregular Comparatives

One should take careful note of the following irregular comparatives since they occur frequently

αγαθος (good) / κρεισσων (better)

κακος (bad) / χειρων (worse)

μεγας (great) / μειζων (greater)

πολυς (much, many) / πλειων (more)

μικρος (small, little) / μικροτερος (smaller, less) / ελαχιστος (smallest, least)

Adverbs

These are formed from the genitive plural -ων by changing the 'ν' to an 'ς'.

καλος (good) / καλως (well)

ομοιος (like) / ομοιως (similarly)

αληθης (true) / αληθως (truly)

ουτος (this) / ουτως (thus)

The comparative is formed from the neuter single of the adjective:

δικαιως (righteous) : δικαιοτερον (more righteous)

While the superlative is formed from the neuter plural:

δικαιως (righteous) : δικαιοτατα (most righteous)

Note: The adverb μαλλον is frequently used to mean more.

Examples

παντων υμων μαλλον γλωσσαις λαλω : I speak in tongues, more than all of you.

In this case μαλλον qualifies the verb λαλω, while in the following example πλειων qualifies the noun δουλους.

απεστειλεν αλλους δουλους πλειονας των πρωτω : He sent other slaves, more than the first.

Note: The comparative often functions in the roll of the superlative:

μειζων δε τουτων η αγαπη : And the greatest of these is love.

Note: When comparing two things, the most common construction is to put the second item which is being compared in the genitive case. However sometimes 'η' (than) is used instead, in which case the two items being compared are put in the same case:

γη Σοδομων ανεκτοτερον εσται εν ημερα κρισεωσ η σοι (Matt 11:24) It will be more tolerable on the day of judgement for the land of Sodom than for you.

Exercises

1. The younger of the sons did not wish to work for (on behalf of) his father.
2. Woe to you, hypocrite. You go and do similarly.
3. Their enemies were more than they.
4. For he is stronger than all the kings of the earth.
5. Why are you going to Jerusalem? Surely Jesus is not greater than Abraham?
6. Behold, hope and love are greater than faith, especially love.
7. This good man did all things well.
8. We must obey the king rather than the priest.

1. Ο νεωτερος των υιων ουκ ηθελεν εργαζεσθαι υπερ του πατρος αυτου.
2. ουσαι σοι, υποκριτα. πορευου και συ ποιει ομοιως.
3. οι εχθροι αυτων ησαν πλειονες αυτων.
4. ουτος γαρ ισχυροτερος εστιν παντων των βασιλεων της γης.
5. τις ερχη εις τα Ιεροσολυμα; ο Ιησους μη εστιν μειζων του Αβρααμ;
6. ιδου η ελπις και η αγαπη μειζονες εστιν της πιστεως, μαλιστα η αγαπη.
7. ουτος αγαθος ανηρ εποιει παντα καλως.
8. δει ημας υπακουειν τω βασιλει μαλλον η τω ιερει.

Vocabulary

μικρος	small
ελαχιστος	smallest
μαλλον	more, rather
μαλιστα	most
αληθως	truly
καλως	well
ομοιως	similarly
ουτως	in this manner, thus
αμην	truly
ευαγγελιζομαι	well
ναι	yes
ουσαι	alas, woe

Perfect and Pluperfect

The perfect has a rather different meaning than the simple tenses such has the present tense (a continuous or repeated action - e.g. I am going *or* I go), the aorist tense (single past event - e.g. I went) or the future tense (e.g. I will go).

Instead the perfect represents a current state resulting from a past action. For example the Greek word γραπω (I wrote) in the perfect tense is γεγραπται. This could be translated as 'it has been written' or 'it was written and now bears witness in the present'. Clearly the second translation is an over-translation, but it captures the full meaning.

When translating into English often the aorist is used instead of the Greek perfect. For example the sentence "Christ died and was raised" Χριστος απεθανεν και εγηγερται (1 Cor 15:3), uses aorist for both verbs in the translation when in fact the Greek word 'raises' implies that Christ is still risen today.

The pluperfect is the same concept as the perfect, but it is shifted back in time a degree. This means that not only was the action performed in the past, but its resulting effect lasted some time in the past, but at present it is finished. The following example uses βαλλω (I throw/place) in the pluperfect:

Λαζαρος εβεβλητο προς τον πυλων αυτου. (Lazarus had been put at his gate) (Luke 16:20)

For the verb λυω the conjugation for the indicative, active, is as follows:

Perfect	Pluperfect
λελυκα	(ε)λελυκειν
λελυκας	(ε)λελυκεις
λελυκε(ν)	(ε)λελυκει
λελυκαμεν	(ε)λελυκειμεν
λελυκατε	(ε)λελυκειτε
λελυκασι(ν)	(ε)λελυκεισαν

Infinitive: λελυκεναι

For the middle and passive it is:

Perfect	Pluperfect

λελυμαι	(ε)λελυμην
λελυσαι	(ε)λελυσο
λελυται	(ε)λελυτο
λελυμεθα	(ε)λελυμεθα
λελυσθε	(ε)λελυσθε
λελυνται	(ε)λελυντο

Infinitive: λελυκεσθαι

The perfect form of λε-λυ-κ-α is made up of:

1. The reduplication

2. The stem

3. κ

4. The conjugated ending

Note: The endings of the perfect are similar to the aorist and the pluperfect are similar to the aorist endings of -βαινω. The middle/passive voice has the same endings as δυναμαι.

Reduplication

134

Reduplication is generally done by repeating the first letter followed by an ε: λυω → λελυκα.

For the letters χ,φ,θ the reduplication is slightly different χ → κεχ, φ → πεφ,θ → τεθ.

If the verb begins with σ,ζ or ξ then ε is prefixed instead (e.g. ζητεω → εζητηκα ; ακολουθεω → ηκολουθηκα) although there are exceptions e.g. σωζω → σεσωκα. If the verb starts with a vowel then this is usually lengthened, e.g. αιτεω → ητηκα.

Note: Some verbs do not have "κ" after the stem and are known as second or strong perfects, e.g. γραφω → γεγραφα

Note: For verbs ending in -εω the ε lengthens to η, e.g. φιλεω → πεφιληκα.

Principle Parts

Although there are basic rules by which the perfect and pluperfect are formed, the stem can be quite different from the present stem. This in fact can be true of any tense of a verb. So to fully know a verb, one must have what are called, 'the principle parts' (PP).

The principle parts consist of the following:

1. Present Active
2. Future Active

3. Aorist Active
4. Perfect Active
5. Perfect Passive
6. Aorist Passive

So far we have encountered all of these, save the last one, which will be covered in the next chapter. For regular verbs such as, λυω and φιλεω the PP are:

λυω λυσω ελυσα λελυκα λελυμαι ελυθην
φιλεω φιλησω εφιλησα πεφιληκα πεφιλημαι εφιληθην

Further tables of PP of verbs are available in the second appendix.

Exercises

1.   He has not injured you or your friends.

2.   Jude, you must proclaim the things which you have heard.

3.   The slaves of the ruler have done the work.

4.   And he answered, 'What I have written, I have written.'

5.   See the place where the body lay.

1.   ουκ ἠδικηκεν σε ἠ τους φιλους σου.

2.   Ιουδα, δει σε κηρυσσειν τα ταυτα ἁ ακηκοας.

3.   οι δουλοι του αρχοντος πεποιηκασιν το εργον.

4.   ο δε απεκρινατο, Ὁ γεγραφα, γεγραφα.

5.   ιδετε τον τοπον οπου εκειο το σωμα.

Vocabulary

These verbs are present in meaning but perfect in form.

οιδα – I know

ηδειν – I knew

ειδεναι – to know

ειδως, ειδυια, ειδος – I was knowing

ειδοτα (participle)

ειδω (subjunctive) – I may know

Deponent Verbs

καθημαι - I sit

κειμαι - I lie

κάθημαι – I sit at table

ανάκειμαι – I sit up at the table

συνανάκειμαι – I sit up at the table with

The Aorist and Future Passives

Like the active form there is both a first and second form of the passive aorist. For the verb λυω this is ελυθην. This can be broken down into: ε-λυ-θ-ην. The parts are augment - stem - θ - (ending of -εβην, aorist of -βαινω). The second or strong forms are the same, but lack the letter θ.

The declension for the first and second Aorist is:

First Aorist Passive	Second Aorist Passive
ελυθην – I was loosed	εγραφην – I was written
ελυθης	εγραφης
ελυθη	εγραφη
ελυθημεν	εγραφημεν
ελυθητε	εγραφητε
ελυθησαν	εγραφησαν

Passive Aorist Imperative forms

λυθητι – be loosed	σπαρηθι – be sown

λυθητω	σπαρητω
λυθητε	σπαρητε
λυθητωσαν	σπαρητωσαν
Infinitive	
λυθηναι – to be loosed	γραφηναι – to be written

The Future Passive is formed in a similar way as the aorist. Using λυω as an example we have, λυ-θησ-(present passive endings). Again the second aorist lacks the θ.

The full conjugation for λυω is given below:

λυθησομαι
λυθηση
λυθησεται
λυθησομεθα
λυθησεσθε
λυθησονται

In the first passive forms, when the letter θ is placed beside certain letters changes occur in the verb stem according to the following rules:

κ, γ, χ + θ → χθ

π, β, φ + θ → φθ

τ, δ, θ + θ → σθ

Examples

- αγω → ηχθην
- πρασσω → επραχθην
- πεμπω→ εμεμφθην

There are numerous irregular forms. Some of which we list here:

Verbs with Irregular Passive First Aorists

ακουω	ηκουσθην

βαλλω	εβληθην
εγειρω	ηγερθην
καλεω	εκληθην
λαμβανω	ελημφθην

Verbs with Irregular Passive Second Aorists

γραφω	εγραφην
σπειρω	εσπαρην
αποστελλω	απεσταλην
κρυπτω	εκρυβην

Exercises

1.   Many of these words were written in a book by the high priest.

2.   The fish were taken by these boys.

3.   We were sown in tribulation, we shall be raised in power.

1. πολλα των ρηματων τουτων εγραφη εν βιβλιω υπο του αρχιερεως.

2. οι ιχθυες ελημφθησαν υπο των παιδων τουτων.

3. εσπαρημεν εν θλυψει εγερθησομεθα εν δυναμει.

Vocabulary

στρεφω (εστραφην - 2nd Aorist Pass.)	I turn
επιστρεφω	I overturn
υποστρεφω	I return
φαινω (εφανην - 2nd Aorist Pass.)	I shine, appear (pass.)

Participles

Participles are common in English with 'ing' words such as, 'rejoicing' and 'laughing'. They can function as adjectives in expressions like, 'the rejoicing student'. Or they may function as a verb, e.g. 'While rejoicing, the student left.'

In Greek, as an adjective, the participle must agree in number, gender and case with the noun it modifies. As a verb it has a voice, tense and potentially an object.

There are four types of participles whose endings fall into either the first, second or third declension.

Type 1

Using λuω as our example *a) the present* form 'loosing' would be

	M sng.	F sng.	N sng.	M plur.	F plur.	N plur.
N	λuων	λuοντα	λuον	λuοντες	λuονται	λuοντα
A	λuοντα	λuονταν	λuον	λuοντας	λuοντας	λuοντα
G	λuοντος	λuοντης	λuοντος	λuοντων	λuοντων	λuοντων
D	λuοντι	λuοντη	λuοντι	λuουσι(v)	λuονταις	λuουσι(v)

Note: The M/N follow the third declension and the F the first declension, so all that needs to be memorized is:

λυων, λυοντα, λυον, λυοντα (the first 4 elements)

and the rest follows.

Note: Observe the contraction οντ + σιν → ουσιν for the dative plural.

There are two other forms that have the type 1 category endings:

b) Second Aorist Active:

βαλων, βαλοντα, βαλον, βαλοντα

c) Present of ειμι

ὠν, ὀντα, ὀν, ὀντα

Type 2

Only the first aorist falls into the type 2 category.

The 1st aorist "having loosed":

λυσας	λυσασα	λυσαν	λυσαντες	λυσασαι	λυσαντα
λυσαντα	λυσασαν	λυσαν	λυσαντας	λυσασας	λυσαντα
λυσαντος	λυσασης	λυσαντος	λυσαντων	λυσασων	λυσαντων

| λυσαντι | λυσαση | λυσαντι | λυσασι(ν) | λυσασαις | λυσασι(ν) |

Note: These endings are the same as παν.

Type 3

This type includes the first and second aorist passive:

λυθεις (having been loosed)

λυθεις	λυθεισα	λυθεν	λυθεντες	λυθεισαι	λυθεντα
λυθεντα	λυθεισαν	λυθεν	λυθεντας	λυθεισας	λυθεντα
λυθεντος	λυθεισης	λυθεντος	λυθεντων	λυθεισων	λυθεντων
λυθεντι	λυθειση	λυθεντι	λυθεισι(ν)	λυθεισαις	λυθεισι(ν)

The second aorist form is the same but lacks the letter 'θ'. For γραφω: the first four elements are:

γραφεις, γραφεισα, γραφεν, γραφεντα

Type 4

Perfect Tense Participle - 'having been loosed'

λελυκως	λελυκυια	λελυκος	λελυκοντες	λελυκυιαι	λελυκοντα
λελυκοντα	λελυκυιαν	λελυκος	λελυκοντας	λελυκυιας	λελυκοντα

λελυκοντος	λελυκυιας	λελυκοντος	λελυκοντων	λελυκυιων	λελυκοντων
λελυκοντι	λελυκυια	λελυκοντι	λελυκουσι(ν)	λελυκυιαις	λελυκουσι(ν)

Participles having First and Second Declension Endings

The rest of the participles have first and second declension endings whose endings are the same as any adjective like αγαπητος -η -ον (beloved).

These endings take the form:

-μενος, -μενη, -μενον

The following voices and tenses fall into this category:

a) Present middle / passive (M/P) (having loosed)

λυομενος, -η, -ον

b) First aorist M (having loosed)

λυσαμενος -η -ον

c) Perfect M/P (having been loosed)

λελυμενος -η -ον

d) Second aorist M (having become)

γενομενος -η -ον

e) δυναμαι (being able)

δυναμενος -η -ον

Uses

As an adjective (articular participle)

In English, one may speak of "the poor" or "the ones lacking speech". Greek has the same forms. E.g.:

οι πιστευοντες (the ones believing)

ο παρα οδος σπειρων (the one who sows by the path)

Notice in the last phrase that there are a number of words between the article and the participle. Often one will find such constructions with entire qualifying phrases between the article and the participle.

As an adverb

There is no article in this case. Rather the participle acts as part of a clause that modifies the main verb. Here we give examples where the participle acts in a temporal and causal form:

Temporal Clauses Examples

και εξελθων ειδεν πολυν οχλον (Matt 14:14) – and having come out, he saw a great crowd και ακουσαντες οι αρχιεριες και οι Φαρισαιοι τας παραβολας αυτου εγνωσαν οτι περι αυτων λεγει (Matt 21:45) And having heard the parables of him, the chief priest and Pharisees knew that he was speaking about them.

Causal Clauses Example

και παντες εφοβουντο αυτον, μη πιστευοντες οτι εστιν μαθητης (Acts 9:26) And they were all afraid of him, because they did not believe that he was a disciple.

Tenses

Generally the tense of the participle is relative to the main verb. So the present participle refers to an action occurring at the same time as the main verb, while an Aorist one would refer to an action occurring before it (temporal clauses are good examples of this).

In some cases where the aorist is used to describe an event occurring at the same time as the main verb. This is known as an 'attendant circumstance', which can be seen in the following common New Testament phrase:

αποκριθεις ειπεν – he answered and said.

Exercises

1.   And having come to the sea of Galilee the disciples taught many people.

2.   Blessed are those that hear and those that believe the words of this book.

3.   Many of the publicans therefore were baptized repenting of their sings.

1.   και ελθοντες προς την θαλασσαν της Γαλιλαιας, οι μαθηται εδιδαξαν πολλους.

2.   μακαριοι οι ακουοντες και οι πιστευοντες τοις λογοις του βιβλιου τουτου.

3.   πολλοι ουν των τελωνων εβαπτισθησαν, μετανοουντες απο των αμαρτιων αυτων.

Genitive Absolute and Periphrastic tenses

Genitive Absolute

Consider the sentence, 'As they ate, he spoke.' This example has two clauses 'as they ate', and 'he spoke', which are unconnected to each other. The first is called a nominative absolute.

In Greek this 'loosed off', unconnected clause, is called the genitive absolute, since it is usually in the genitive. An example of this would be:

και πορευομενων αυτων εν τη οδω ειπεν τις προς αυτον (Luke 9:57) – And as they were going in the way, a certain man said to him.

In the following examples the genitive absolute is not used, since both clauses are related to the main verb.

εξελθων ειδεν – When he had come out, he saw. (Nominative role for the participle)

τον Πετρον εξερχομαενον ειδεν ο Ιησους – As Peter came out, Jesus saw him. (Accusative role for the participle)

However the NT authors do not always follow the grammatical rules strictly:

εκπορευομενου αυτου εκ του ιερου λεγει αυτω εις τνω μαθητων αυτου (Mark 13:1)

Periphrastic Tenses

The Greek words, περι (round/about) and φραζω (point out/show) give us the word periphrastic. The periphrastic tense uses the verb 'to be' (ειμι) with another verb to express a tense. Here we give examples of the different tenses being used:

Periphrastic Imperfect: και ην προαγων αυτους ο Ιησους (Mark 10:32) - And Jesus was going ahead of them.

Future: απο του νυν ανθρωπους έση ζωυρων (Luke 5:10) - From now on you will catch men.

Perfect: χαριτι εστε σεσωσμενοι (Eph 2:5) - By grace you have been saved.

Pluperfect: και ην ο 'Ιωανης ενδεδυμενος τιρχος καμηλου (Mark 1:6) - And John was clothed with camel's hair.

In the case of the **perfect** the present of ειμι is used with the perfect particle, while to give a **pluperfect** tense, the imperfect of ειμι is used with the perfect particle.

Exercises

1. And when the disciples had entered into the boat Jesus sent the multitudes into the mountains.

2. And a certain man came to him and said, 'What are you doing here?'

3. What power shall we receive when the Holy Spirit has come upon us?

4. When the day has drawn near the Son of man will come with the clouds of heaven.

5. But Peter came to him walking upon the water.

1. Εισελυοντων δε των μαθητων εις το πλοιον απεστειλεν ο Ἰησους τα πληθη εις τα ορη.

2. και τις ανθρωπος ελθων προς αυτον ειπεν, Τί ποιεις ωδε;

3. Τίνα δυναμιν λημψομεθα ελθοντος του Ἁγιο Πνευματος εφ' ημας;

4. της ημερας εγγισασης ο Υιος του ανθρωπου ελευσεται μετα τνω νεφελων του ουρανου.

5. ο δε Πετρος ελθεν προς αυτον περιπατων επι το υδωρ.

Vocabulary

οσος -η -ον	as much as; pl., as many as.
τοιουτος -αυτη -ουτο	of such kind
ποιος -α -ον	of what sort? what?
ὡδε	here
ἐκει	there
ὁπου	where
ἐγγυς	near

The Subjunctive Mood

The subjunctive is a mood of doubtful assertion. This occurs in English most commonly with fictional situations, e.g. 'If I were eighteen, I would eat that whole pizza.'.

In the Greek of the New Testament the subjective is very commonly used. Fortunately it differs little from the indicative, as one can see in the table below:

Present Subjective

active	middle/passive
λυω	λυωμαι
λυῃς	λυῃ
λυῃ	λυηται
λυωμεν	λυωμεθα
λυητε	λυησθε
λυωσι(ν)	λυωνται

Note: The initial vowel of the ending is lengthened and the iota is written as a subscript for η.

The endings in the table above apply to a number of other tenses.

Tenses with the Same Endings as the Present Active

1. Subjunctive of ειμι: ω

2. Subjunctive of οιδα: ειδω
3. First Aorist Active: λυσω
4. Second Aorist Active: βαλω
5. First Aorist Passive: λυθω
6. Second Aorist Passive: γραφω

Tenses with the Same Endings as the Present Middle/Passive

1. First Aorist Middle: λυσωμαι
2. Second Aorist Middle: γενωμαι

Where the Subjunctive is Used

Indefinite Clauses

There are a number of elements that can make a clause become indefinite: (1) the person, (2) the time or (3) the place. Often the particle 'αν' is included to reinforce this indefiniteness.

- For an indefinite person the relative pronoun (ος or οστις) is used with αν.
- For place or time οπου or οτε (where) is used with 'αν' where οτε+αν → οταν.
- Until (εως) is also used for indefiniteness.

Examples

- ος αν θελη εν υμιν ειναι πρωτος : Whoever wishes to be first among you
- ακολουθησω σοι οπου εαν απερχη : I will follow you wherever you go.

- οπου εαν εισλθητε εις οικιαν, εκει μενετε εως αν εξελθητε : Wherever you go into into a house, there stay until you go out.

Note: There is no indefiniteness if the phrase refers to a past event. E.g. οπου αν εισεπορευτο : Whenever he entered

Purposes Clauses

These clauses are generally introduced with the words, ινα or οπως. ινα can also be used in noun clauses either as a subject or object of a verb

Examples

- μη κρινετε, ινα μη κριθητε : Do not judge, lest you be judged.
- ειπε ινα οι λιθοι ουτοι αρτοι γενωνται: Tell these stones to become bread
- εμον βρωμα εστιν ινα ποιω το θελμηα του πεμπψαντος με : To do the will of him who sent me is my food.

Exhorting others

Example: φαωμεν και πιωμεν, αυριον γαρ αποθνησκομεν : Let us eat and drink, for tomorrow we die!

Double Negative Future

When both 'ou' and 'μη' are used with the future, the tense becomes subjunctive.

Example: αμεν, λεγω οτι ου μη παρελθη η γενεα αυτη εως αν παντα ταυτα γενηται : Amen, I say to you that this generation will not pass away until all these things come to be.

Deliberating Questions

Example: τι ουν ποιησωμεν; : What then should we do?

A Command Not to Begin a Action

Example: μη μου απτου : Do not continue to hold me.

A Future Condition

This uses the indefinite if: ει + αν → εαν.

Example: εαν μονον αψωμαι αυτον : If only I touch him

Exercsies

1. Truly, I say to you, he will not see until the age to come.
2. What am I to say to you
3. In order that you bear fruit

1. αμην, λεγω υμιν, θανατον ου μη θεωρηση εις τον αιωνα
2. τι ειπω υμιν
3. ινα καρπον πολυν φερητε

The Optative Mood

The Optative mood was an important part of the grammar of ancient Greek before the time of Alexander the Great. Since his conquests in 333 BC, its use has been in decline. So while it is found in the Septuigent (the Greek Old Testiment), it rarely appears in the New Testament. When it does appear it is usually in certain expressions such as: μη γενοιτο (may it not be!). Note that μη is used to negate the verb in the Optative mood.

Generally the optative mood may be characterized as the mood of doubtful assertion. The conjugation for λυω follows:

Present Optative

active	middle/passive
λύοιμι	λυοίμην
λύοις	λύοιο
λύοι	λύοιτο
λύοιμεν	λυοίμεθα
λύοιτε	λύοισθε
λύοιεν	λύοιντο

Note: There is a characteristic 'οι' before the endings.

Often the optative is used with αν (particle which expresses doubt) or εἰ (if).

Examples

- αλλ' ει πασχοιτε δια δικαιοσυνην : but if you might suffer for righteousness (1 Peter 3:14)
- πως γαρ αν δυναιημν : for how would I be able (Acts 8:31)

Exercsies

1. What would this one wish to say?
2. May *I* take from you?
3. May the God of peace loose you (pl.).

1. τι αν θελοι ουτος λεγιεν;
2. εγω σου λαμβανοιμι;
3. ο θεος της ειρηνης λυοι υμας.

Verbs ending in -αω and -οω

Previously we dealt with ending contractions for -εω verbs such as φιλεω (I love). In this chapter we look at verbs that end in -αω or -οω. Two such examples are the verbs τιμαω (I honor) and φανεροω (I make clear).

The principle parts of these verbs are:

φιλεω	φιλησω	εφιλησα	πεφιληκα	πεφιλημαι	εφιληθην
τιμαω	τιμησω	ετιμησα	τετιμηκα	τετιμημαι	ετιμηθην
φανεροω	φανερωσω	εφανερωσα	πεφανερωκα	πεφανερωμαι	εφανερωθην

Note: α lengthens to η, and o to ω.

When conjugating -αω and -οω verbs contractions occur according to the following rules:

α + O-sound (o, ω or ου) → ω

α + E-sound (ε or η) → α

α + any combination containing ι → ᾳ

o + long vowel → ω

o + short vowel → ου

o + any combination containing ι → οι

The only apparent exceptions are the infinitives (-ειν): τιμᾳν and φανερουν (not τιμᾳν and φανεροιν). This is because ειν is a contraction of εεν. If the uncontracted ending is used, then the correct infinitives are formed according to the rules above.

Note: The verb ζαω (I live) is a true exception and has the present tense conjugation: ζω ζης ζη ζωμεν ζητε ζωσιν

Exercises

1.   The disciples were making known these things which they had heard.

2.   Do not continue to crucify slaves.

3.   Are they about to live in our city?

4.   Do you then wish to love the Lord your God?

1.   οι μαθηται εφανερουν ταυτα ἁ ηκουσαν.

2.   μη σταυρουτε δουλους.

3.   μελλουσιν ζην εν τη πολει ἡμων;

4.   θελετε ἁρα αγαπαν Κυριον τον Θεον ὑμων;

Vocabulary

αγαπαω	I love
γενναω	I beget

162

ερωταω	I ask, question
επερωταω	I ask, question
οραω	I see
πλαναω	I cause to wander
τιμαω	I honour
επιτιμαω	I rebuke/ warn
καυχαομαι	I boast
ζαω	I live
δικαιοω	I justify
πληροω	I fill
σταυροω	I crucify
φανεροω	I make clear

-μι verbs and the verb τιθημι

Verbs which end in μι differ from -ω verbs in the Present, Imperfect and Second Aorist tenses. They are conjugated from either the verbal or present stem.

		Verbal stem	Present Stem
τιθημι	I place	θε	τιθε
διδωμι	I give	δο	διδο
ιστημι	I cause to stand	στα	ιστα

Note: The present stem is a reduplication of the verbal stem.

The principle parts of τιθημι are:

τιθημι, θησω, εθηκα, τεθεικα, τεθειμαι, ετεθην

Present Active

Indicative	Subjunctive	Participle	Imperative	Infinitive
τιθημι	τιθω	τιθεις -εισα -εν		τιθεναι
τιθης	τιθης	τιθεντα	τιθει	

τιθησι(ν)	τιθη		τιθετω	
τιθεμεν	τιθωμεν			
τιθετε	τιθητε		τιθετε	
τιθεασι(ν)	τιθωσι(ν)		τιθετωσαν	

The middle and passive have the same endings as λυω.

Middle and Passive: τιθεμαι, τιθεμενος, τιθεσθαι

The First Aorist is formed regularly in the indicative. The Second Aorist Middle has the same meaning as the First Active Aorist.

Aorist Active

Indicative	Subjunctive	Participle	Imperative	Infinitive
εθηκα	θω	θεις -εισα -εν		θειναι
εθηκας	θης	θεντα	θες	
εθηκεν	θη		θετω	
εθηκαμεν	θωμεν			
εθηκατε	θητε		θετε	

εθηκαν	θωσι(ν)		θετωσαν	

Second Aorist Middle:

εθεμην

εθου

εθετο

εθεμεθα

εθεσθε

εθεντο

Exercises

1. We must place the law of love in our hearts daily
2. Place joy there similarly
3. Where have you laid him?
4. How shall we place our daughter at his feet?

1. δει ημας τιθεναι τον νομον της αγαπης εν ταις καρδιαις ημων
   καθ' ημεραν.
2. τιθετε εκει την χαραν ομοιως.
3. που τεθεικατε αυτον;
4. πως θωμεν την θυγατερα ημων παρα τους ποδας αυτον;

Vocabulary

δıδημι	I place
επιτιθημι	I place upon

The Verb διδωμι

διδωμι has a similar conjugation to τιθημι, except that θε is replaced by δο and ου instead of ει. Also there is an ω in the subjunctive endings.

Principle Parts: διδωμι, δωσω, εδωκα, δεδωκα, δεδομαι, εδοθην

Present Active

Indicative	Subjunctive	Participle	Imperative	Infinitive
διδωημι	διδω	διδους -ουσα -ον		διδοναι
διδως	διδῳς	διδοντα	διδου	
διδωσι(ν)	διδῳ		διδοτω	
διδομεν	διδωμεν			
διδοτε	διδωτε		διδοτε	
διδοασι(ν)	διδωσι(ν)		διδοτωσαν	

Middle and Passive: διδομαι, διομενος, διδοσθαι

168

Aorist Active

Indicative	Subjunctive	Participle	Imperative	Infinitive
First Aorist	δω	δους -ουσα -ον		δουναι
	δῳς	δοντα	δος	
	δῳ		δοτω	
	δωμεν			
	δωτε		δοτε	
	δωσι(ν)		δοτωσαν	

Second Aorist Middle:

εδομην

εδου

εδοτο

εδομεθα

εδοσθε

169

εδοντο

Exercises

1.   Always pay all that you have.

2.   Give to the poor today.

3.   We wish to give it to the high-priests.

4.   It was given to me by my father.

1. Παντοτε αποδιδου παντα ἀ ἐχεις.
2. σημερον δος τοις πτωχοις.
3. θελομεν δουναι τοις αρχιερευσιν.
4. εδοθη μοι υπο του πατρος μου.

Vocabulary

διδωμι	I give
αποδιδωμι	I give back, pay; Middle: sell
παραδιδωμι	I had over, betray

The verb ιστημι

The verb ιστημι (I cause to stand) has the unusual property of having different forms depending whether it is used transitively or intransitively. Also the perfect tense has the same meaning as the present and the pluperfect the same as the imperfect.

The principle parts are:

Transitive	ιστημι	στησω	εστησα			
Intransitive			εστην	εστηκα	-	εσταθην

The Full conjugations in the active are:

Present Active

Indicative	Subjunctive	Participle	Infinitive
ιστημι	ιστω	ιστας ιστασα ισταν	ισταναι
ιστης	ιστῃς	ισταντα	
ιστησι(ν)	ιστῃ		
ισταμεν	ιστωμεν		

ιστατε	ιστητε		
ιστασι(ν)	ιστωσι(ν)		

Middle and Passive: ισταμαι, ισταμενος, ιστασθαι

Aorist Active

Indicative	Subjunctive	Participle	Infinitive
εστην	στω	στας στασα σταν	στηναι
εστης	στῃς	σταντα	
εστη	στῃ		
εστημεν	στωμεν		
εστητε	στητε		
εστησαν	στωσι(ν)		

Exercises

1. I will cause you to stand in darkness

2. There are certain of those stand here.

3. Paul therefore must stand in the council

4. The priests stood the publican there.

1. στησω σε εν σκοτει.

2. εισιν τινες των ωδε εστωτων.

3. ουν δει τον Παυλον στηναι εν τω συνεδριω.

4. οι ιερεις εστησαν εκει τον τελωνην.

Vocabulary

ιστημι	I cause to stand
ανιστημι	I raise up
εφιστημι	I stand over, come upon
καθιστημι	I appoint
παριστημι	I cause to stand beside

Appendix A: Grammar Tables

The Article

	Masculine		Feminine		Neuter	
	Singular	Plural	Singular	Plural	Singular	Plural
Nominative	ὁ	οἱ	ἡ	αἱ	τό	τά
Genitive	τοῦ	τῶν	τῆς	τῶν	τοῦ	τῶν
Dative	τῷ	τοῖς	τῇ	ταῖς	τῷ	τοῖς
Accusative	τόν	τούς	τήν	τάς	τό	τά

Masculine Examples ending with -ας or -ης

	νεανίας		στρατιώτης	
	Singular	Plural	Singular	Plural
Nominative	νεανίᾱς	νεανίαι	στρατιώτης	στρατιῶται
Genitive	νεανίου	νεανιῶν	στρατιώτου	στρατιωτῶν
Dative	νεανίᾳ	νεανίαις	στρατιώτῃ	στρατιώταις
Accusative	νεανίᾱν	νεανίᾱς	στρατιώτην	στρατιώτᾱς
Vocative	νεανίᾱ	νεανίαι	στρατιῶτᾰ	στρατιῶται

Second Declension Noun Examples

	Masculine		Feminine		Neuter	
	ἄνθρωπος		ὁδός		δῶρον	
	Singular	Plural	Singular	Plural	Singular	Plural
Nominative	ἄνθρωπος	ἄνθρωποι	ὁδός	ὁδοί	δῶρον	δῶρα
Genitive	ἀνθρώπου	ἀνθρώπων	ὁδοῦ	ὁδῶν	δώρου	δώρων
Dative	ἀνθρώπῳ	ἀνθρώποις	ὁδῷ	ὁδοῖς	δώρῳ	δώροις
Accusative	ἄνθρωπον	ἀνθρώπους	ὁδόν	ὁδούς	δῶρον	δῶρα
Vocative	ἄνθρωπε	ἄνθρωποι	ὁδέ	ὁδοί	δῶρον	δῶρα

Relative Pronouns

	Masculine		Feminine		Neuter	
	Singular	Plural	Singular	Plural	Singular	Plural
Nominative	ὅς	οἵ	ἥ	αἵ	ὅ	ἅ
Genitive	οὗ	ὧν	ἧς	ὧν	οὗ	ὧν
Dative	ᾧ	οἷς	ᾗ	αἷς	ᾧ	οἷς
Accusative	ὅν	οὕς	ἥν	ἅς	ὅ	ἅ

The Full Declension of the Verb ειμι

	Indicative	Subjunctive	Optative	Imperative	Infinitive	Participle
Present	εἰμί	ὦ	εἴην	-	εἶναι	ὤν
	εἶ	ᾖς	εἴης	ἴσθι		οὖσα

174

ἐστί(ν)	ἦ	εἴη	ἔστω		ὄν
ἐσμέν	ὦμεν	εἴημεν/	-		
ἐστέ	ἦτε	εἶμεν	ἔστε		
εἰσί(ν)	ὦσι	εἴητε/εἶτε	ἔστων/ὄντων/		
		εἴησαν/εἶεν	ἔστωσαν		

Imperfect
ἦν
ἦσθα
ἦν
ἦμεν
ἦτε
ἦσαν

ἔσομαι	ἐσοίμην			
ἔσῃ/ἔσει	ἔσοιο			ἐσόμενος
ἔσται	ἔσοιτο	ἔσεσθαι		ἐσομένη
ἐσόμεθα	ἐσοίμεθα			ἐσόμενον
ἔσεσθε	ἔσοισθε			

Future ἔσονται   ἔσοιντο

The Active Voice of λυω

	Indicative	Subjunctive	Optative	Imperative	Infinitive	Participle
	λύω	λύω	λύοιμι	-		
	λύεις	λύῃς	λύοις	λῦε		λύων
	λύει	λύῃ	λύοι	λυέτω		λύουσα
	λύομεν	λύωμεν	λύοιμεν	-	λύειν	λῦον
	λύετε	λύητε	λύοιτε	λύετε		
Present	λύουσι(ν)	λύωσι(ν)	λύοιεν	λυόντων/ λυέτωσαν		
	ἔλυον					
	ἔλυες					
	ἔλυε(ν)					
	ἐλύομεν					
	ἐλύετε					
Imperfect	ἔλυον					
	λύσω		λύσοιμι			
	λύσεις		λύσοις			λύσων
	λύσει		λύσοι		λύσειν	λύσουσα
	λύσομεν		λύσοιμεν			λῦσον
	λύσετε		λύσοιτε			
Future	λύσουσι(ν)		λύσοιεν			
Aorist	ἔλυσα	λύσω	λύσαιμι	-	λῦσαι	λύσας
	ἔλυσας	λύσῃς	λύσαις/	λῦσον		λύσασα
	ἔλυσε	λύσῃ	λύσειας	λυσάτω		λῦσαν
	ἐλύσαμεν	λύσωμεν	λύσαι/	-		
	ἐλύσατε	λύσητε	λύσειε	λύσατε		
	ἔλυσαν	λύσωσι	λύσαιμεν	λυσάντων/ λυσάτωσαν		
			λύσαιτε			

	Indicative	Subjunctive	Optative	Imperative	Infinitive	Participle
Perfect	λέλυκα λέλυκας λέλυκε λελύκαμεν λελύκατε λελύκασι	λελυκώς ὦ λελυκώς ᾖς λελυκώς ᾖ λελυκότες ὦμεν λελυκότες ἦτε λελυκότες ὦσι	λύσαιεν/ λύσειαν λελυκώς εἴην λελυκώς εἴης λελυκώς εἴη λελυκότες εἴημεν λελυκότες εἴητε λελυκότες εἴησαν	- λελυκώς ἴσθι λελυκώς ἔστω - λελυκότες ἔστε λελυκότες ἔστων	λελυκέναι	λελυκώς λελυκυῖα λελυκός
Pluperfect	ἐλελύκη ἐλελύκης ἐλελύκει(ν) ἐλελύκεμεν ἐλελύκετε ἐλελύκεσαν					
Future Perfect	λελυκώς ἔσομαι λελυκώς ἔσῃ/ἔσει λελυκώς ἔσται λελυκότες ἐσόμεθα λελυκότες ἔσεσθε λελυκότες ἔσονται					

The Middle Voice of λυω

	Indicative	Subjunctive	Optative	Imperative	Infinitive	Participle
Present	λύομαι λύῃ/λύει λύεται λυόμεθα λύεσθε λύονται	λύωμαι λύῃ λύηται λυώμεθα λύησθε λύωνται	λυοίμην λύοιο λύοιτο λυοίμεθα λύοισθε λύοιντο	- λύου λυέσθω - λύεσθε λυέσθων/ λυέσθωσαν	λύεσθαι	λυόμενος λυομένη λυόμενον
Imperfect	ἐλυόμην ἐλύου ἐλύετο ἐλυόμεθα					

έλύεσθε
έλύοντο

	Indicative	Subjunctive	Optative	Imperative	Infinitive	Participle
Future	λύσομαι λύση/λύσει λύσεται λυσόμεθα λύσεσθε λύσονται		λυσοίμην λύσοιο λύσοιτο λυσοίμεθα λύσοισθε λύσοιντο		λύσεσθαι	λυσόμενος λυσομένη λυσόμενον
Aorist	έλυσάμην έλύσω έλύσατο έλυσάμεθα έλύσασθε έλύσαντο	λύσωμαι λύση λύσηται λυσώμεθα λύσησθε λύσωνται	λυσαίμην λύσαιο λύσαιτο λυσαίμεθα λύσαισθε λύσαιντο	- λῦσαι λυσάσθω - λύσασθε λυσάσθων/ λυσάσθωσαν	λύσασθαι	λυσάμενος λυσαμένη λυσάμενον
Perfect	λέλυμαι λέλυσαι λέλυται λελύμεθα λέλυσθε λέλυνται	λελυμένος ὦ λελυμένος ᾖς λελυμένος ᾖ λελυμένοι ὦμεν λελυμένοι ἦτε λελυμένοι ὦσι	λελυμένος εἴην λελυμένος εἴης λελυμένος εἴη λελυμένοι εἴημεν λελυμένοι εἴητε λελυμένοι εἴησαν	- λέλυσο λελύσθω - λέλυσθε λελύσθων/ λελύσθωσαν	λελύσθαι	λελυμένος λελυμένη λελυμένον
Pluperfect	έλελύμην έλέλυσο έλέλυτο έλελύμεθα έλέλυσθε έλέλυντο					
Future Perfect	λελύσομαι λελύση/ λελύσει λελύσεται λελυσόμεθα λελύσεσθε λελύσονται		λελυσοίμην λελύσοιο λελύσοιτο λελυσοίμεθα λελύσοισθε λελύσοιντο		λελύσεσθαι	λελυσόμενος λελυσομένη λελυσόμενον

The Passive Voice of λυω

	Indicative	Subjunctive	Optative	Imperative	Infinitive	Participle
Present	λύομαι λύη/λύει λύεται λυόμεθα	λύωμαι λύη λύηται λυώμεθα	λυοίμην λύοιο λύοιτο λυοίμεθα	- λύου λυέσθω -	λύεσθαι	λυόμενος λυομένη λυόμενον

Tense	Indicative	Subjunctive	Optative	Imperative	Infinitive	Participle
	λύεσθε	λύησθε	λύοισθε	λύεσθε		
	λύονται	λύωνται	λύοιντο	λυέσθων/ λυέσθωσαν		
Imperfect	ἐλυόμην ἐλύου ἐλύετο ἐλυόμεθα ἐλύεσθε ἐλύοντο					
Future	λυθήσομαι λυθήσῃ/ λυθήσει λυθήσεται λυθησόμεθα λυθήσεσθε λυθήσονται		λυθησοίμην λυθήσοιο λυθήσοιτο λυθησοίμεθα λυθήσοισθε λυθήσοιντο		λυθήσεσθαι	λυθησόμενος λυθησομένη λυθησόμενον
Aorist	ἐλύθην ἐλύθης ἐλύθη ἐλύθημεν ἐλύθητε ἐλύθησαν	λυθῶ λυθῇς λυθῇ λυθῶμεν λυθῆτε λυθῶσι	λυθείην λυθείης λυθείη λυθείημεν/ λυθεῖμεν λυθείητε/ λυθεῖτε λυθείησαν/ λυθεῖεν	- λύθητι λυθήτω - λύθητε λυθέντων/ λυθήτωσαν	λυθῆναι	λυθείς λυθεῖσα λυθέν
Perfect	λέλυμαι λέλυσαι λέλυται λελύμεθα λέλυσθε λέλυνται	λελυμένος ὦ λελυμένος ᾖς λελυμένος ᾖ λελυμένοι ὦμεν λελυμένοι ἦτε λελυμένοι ὦσι	λελυμένος εἴην λελυμένος εἴης λελυμένος εἴη λελυμένοι εἴημεν λελυμένοι εἴητε λελυμένοι εἴησαν	- λέλυσο λελύσθω - λέλυσθε λελύσθων/ λελύσθωσαν	λελύσθαι	λελυμένος λελυμένη λελυμένον
Pluperfect	ἐλελύμην ἐλέλυσο ἐλέλυτο ἐλελύμεθα ἐλέλυσθε ἐλέλυντο					
Future Perfect	λελύσομαι λελύσῃ/ λελύσει λελύσεται		λελυσοίμην λελύσοιο λελύσοιτο λελυσοίμεθα		λελύσεσθαι	λελυσόμενος λελυσομένη λελυσόμενον

λελυσόμεθα   λελύσοισθε
λελύσεσθε   λελύσοιντο
λελύσονται

Further tables can be found at the site
'https://en.wikipedia.org/wiki/Ancient_Greek_grammar_(tables)'.

Appendix B: Principle Parts of Common New Testament Verbs

Translation	Present	Future	Aorist A.	Perfect A.	Perfect P.	Aorist P.
lift up	αἴρω	ἀρῶ	ἦρα	ἦρκα	ἦρμαι	ἤρθην
take	αἱρέω	αἱρήσομαι	εἱλόμην	ἥρηκα	ἥρημαι	ἧρέθην
ask for	αἰτέω	αἰτήσω	ᾔτησα	ᾔτηκα	ᾔτημαι	ᾐτήθην
go	-βαίνω	-βήσομαι	-έβην	-βέβηκα	———	-εβήθην
throw	βάλλω	βαλῶ	ἔβαλον	βέβληκα	βέβλημαι	ἐβλήθην
baptize	βαπτίζω	βαπτίσω	ἐβάπτισα	———	βεβάπτισμαι	ἐβαπτίσθην
torment	βασανίζω	βασανιῶ	ἐβασάνισα	———	βαβασάνισμαι	ἐβασανίσθην
cry out	βοάω	βοήσω	ἐβόησα	———	βεβόημαι	ἐβώσθην
marry	γαμέω	γαμήσω	ἐγάμησα	γεγάμηκα	γεγάμημαι	ἐγαμήθην
love	ἀγαπάω	ἀγαπήσω	ἠγάπησα	ἠγάπηκα	ἠγάπημαι	ἠγαπήθην
rise	ἐγείρω	ἐγερῶ	ἤγειρα	ἐγήγερκα	ἐγήγερμαι	ἠγέρθην
beget	γεννάω	γεννήσω	ἐγέννησα	γεγέννηκα	γεγέννημαι	ἐγεννήθην
know	γινώσκω	γνώσομαι	ἔγνων	ἔγνωκα	ἔγνςσμαι	ἐγνώσθην
become	γίνομαι	γενήσομαι	ἐγενόμην	γέγονα	γεγένημαι	ἐγενήθην
ignorant	ἀγνοέω	ἀγνοήσω	ἠγνόησα	ἠγνόηκα	ἠγνόημαι	ἠγνοήθην
make known	γνωρίζω	γνωπίσω	ἐγνώπισα	ἐγνώπικα	———	ἐγνωρίσθην
lead	ἡγέομαι	ἡγήσομαι	ἡγησάμην	———	ἥγημαι	———
buy	ἀγοράζω	ἀγοράσω	ἠγόρασα	ἠγόακα	ἠγόασμαι	ἠγοράσθην
write	γράφω	γράψω	ἔγραψα	γέγραφα	γέγραμμαι	ἐγράφην
lead	ἄγω	ἄξω	ἤγαγον	ἦχα	ἦγμαι	ἤχθην
show	δείκνυμι	δείξω	ἔδειξα	δέδειχα	δέδειγμαι	ἐδείχθην
show	δηλόω	δηλώσω	ἐδήλωσα	δεδήλωκα	δεδήλωμαι	ἐδηλώθην
serve	διακονέω	διακονήσω	διηκόνησα	δεδιηκόνηκα	δεδιακόνημαι	διηκονήθην
discuss	διαλέγομαι	διαλέξομαι	διελεξάμην	———	διείλεγμαι	διελέχθην
tarry	διατρίβω	διατρίψω	διέτριψα	———	διατέτριμμαι	διετρίβην
teach	διδάσκω	διδάξω	ἐδίδαξα	δεδίδαχα	δεδίδαγμαι	ἐδιδάχθην
give	δίδωμι	δώσω	ἔδωκα	δέδωκα	δέδομαι	ἐδόθην
justify	δικαιόω	δικαιώσω	ἐδικαίωσα	———	δεδικαίωμαι	ἐδικαιώθην
do wrong	ἀδικέω	ἀδικήσω	ἠδίκησα	ἠδίκηκα	-	ἠδικήθην
persecute	διώκω	διώξω	ἐδίωξα	δεδίωχα	δεδίωγμαι	ἐδιώχθην
test	δοκιμάζω	δοκιμάσω	ἐδοκίμασα	———	δεδοκίμασμαι	
suppose	δοκέω	δόξω	ἔδοξα	δεδόκηκα	δεδόκημαι	ἐδοκήθην
glorify	δοξάζω	δοξάσω	ἐδόξασα	δεδόξακα	δεδόξασμαι	ἐδοξάσθην
strike	δέρω	———	ἔδειρα	———	δέδαρμαι	ἐδάρην
able	δύναμαι	δυνήσομαι	ἐδυνάμην	———	δεδύνημαι	ἐδυνήθην
receive	δέχομαι	δέξομαι	ἐδεξάμην	———	δέδεγμαι	ἐδέχθην
bind	δέω	δήσω	ἔδησα	δέδεκα	δέδεμαι	ἐδέθην
bestow freely	δωρέομαι	δωρήσω	ἐδωρησάμην	———	δεδώρημαι	ἐδωρήθην
evangelize	εὐαγγελίζω	εὐαγγελίσω	εὐηγγέλισα	εὐηγγέλικα	εὐηγγέλισμαι	εὐηγγλίσθην

bless	εὐλογέω	εὐλογήσω	εὐλόγησα	εὐλόγηκα	εὐλόγημαι	εὐλογήθην
find	εὑρίσκω	εὑρήσω	εὗρον	εὕρηκα	εὕρημαι	εὑρέθην
give thanks	εὐχαριστέω	εὐχαριστήσω	εὐχαρίστησα	εὐχαριστήκα	εὐχαριστήμαι	εὐχαριστήθην
seek	ζητέω	ζητήσω	ἐζήτησα	ἐζήτηκα	———	ἐζητήθην
live	ζάω	ζήσω	ἔζησα	βεβίωκα	———	
tear	ῥήγνυμι	ῥήξω	ἔρρηξα	ἔρρωγα	ἔρρηγμαι	ἐρράγην
bury	θάπτω	θάψω	ἔθψα	———	τέθαμμαι	ἐτάφην
amaze	θαυμάζω	θαυμάσομαι	ἐθαύμασα	τεθαύμακα	τεθαύμασμαι	ἐθαυμάσθην
behold	θεάομαι	θεάσομαι	ἐθεασάμην	———	τεθέαμαι	ἐθεάθην
heal	θεραπεύω	θεραπεύσω	ἐθεράπευσα	τεθεράπευκα	τεθεράπευμαι	ἐθεραπεύθην
afflict	θλίβω	θλίψω	ἔθλιψα		τέθλιμμαι	ἐθλίβην
wish	θέλω	θελήσω	ἠθέλησα	ἠθέληκα	———	ἠθελήθην
sacrifice	θύω	θύσω	ἔθυσα	τέθυκα	τέθυμαι	ἐτύθην
cleanse	καθαρίζω	καθαριῶ	ἐκαθάροσα	———	κεκαθάρισμαι	ἐκαθαρίσθην
burn	καίω	καύσω	ἔκαυσα	κέκαυκα	κέκαυμαι	ἐκαύθην
call	καλέω	καλέσω	ἐκάλεσα	κέκληκα	κέκλημαι	ἐκλήθην
make idle	καταργέω	καταργήσω	κατήργησα	κατήργηκα	κατήργημαι	κατηργήθην
mend	καταρτίζω	καταρτίσω	κατήρτισα	———	κατήρτισμαι	———
prepare	κατασκευάζω	κατασκευάσω	κατεσκεύασα	———	κατεσκεύασμαι	κατεσκεύασθη
boast	καυχάομαι	καυχήσομαι	ἐκαυχησάμην	———	κεκαύχημαι	
order	κελεύω	κελεύσω	ἐκέλευσα	κεκέλευκα	κεκέλευσμαι	ἐκελεύσθην
gain	κερδαίνω	κερδήσω	ἐκέρδησα	κεκέρδηκα	———	ἐκερδήθην
proclaim	κηρύσσω	κηρύξω	ἐκήρυξα	κεκήρυχα	κεκήρυγμαι	ἐκηρύχθην
cut off	ἐκκόπτω	ἐκκόψω	ἐξέκοψα	ἐκκέκοφα	———	ἐξεκόπην
weep	κλαίω	κλαύσω	ἔκλαυσα	———	κέκλαυμαι	ἐκλαύσθην
steal	κλέπτω	κλέψω	ἔκλεψα	κέκλοφα	κέκλεμμαι	ἐκλάπην
shut	κλείω	κλείσω	ἔκλεισα	———	κέκλεισμαι	ἐκλείσθην
bow	κλίνω	κλινῶ	ἔκλινα	κέκλικα	κέκλιμαι	ἐκλίθην
break	κλάω	κλάσω	ἔκλασα	———	κέκλασμαι	ἐκλάσθην
fall asleeep	κοιμάομαι	κοιμήσω	ἐκοίμησα	———	κεκοίμημαι	ἐκοιμήθην
cling	κολλάομαι	κολλήσω	———	———	κεκόλλημαι	ἐκολλήθην
follow	ἀκολουθέω	ἀκολουθήσω	ἠκολούθησα	ἠκολούθηκα	———	———
bring	κομίζω	κομιῶ	ἐκόμισα	κεκόμικα	κεκόμισμαι	ἐκομίσθην
adorn	κοσμέω	κοσμήσω	ἐκόσμησα	———	κεκόσμημαι	
hear	ἀκούω	ἀκούσω	ἤκουσα	ἀκήκοα	ἤκουσμαι	ἠκούσθην
amaze	ἐκπλήσσω	ἐκπλήκω	ἐξέπληξα			ἐξεπλάγην
cry out	κράζω	κράξω	ἔκραξα	κέκραγα		
grasp	κρατέω	κρατήσω	ἐκράτησα	κεκράτηκα	κεκράτημαι	
judge	κρίνω	κρινῶ	ἔκρινα	κέκρικα	κέκριμαι	ἐκρίθην
hide	κρύπτω	κρύψω	ἔκρυψα	κέκρυφα	κέκρυμμαι	ἐκρύβην
stretch out	ἐκτείνω	ἐκτενῶ	ἐκέτεινα	ἐκτέτακα	ἐκτέταμαι	———
create	κτίζω	κτίσω	ἔκτισα	———	ἔκτισμαι	ἐκτίσθην
pour out	ἐκχέω	ἐκχεῶ	ἐξέχεα	———	ἐκκέχυμαι	ἐξεχύθην

forbid	κωλύω	κωλύσω	ἐκώλυσα	κεκώλυκα	κεκώλυμαι	ἐκωλύθην
speak	λαλέω	λαλήσω	ἐλάλησα	λελάληκα	λελάλημαι	ἐλαλήθην
receive	λαμβάνω	λήμψομαι	ἔλαβον	εἴληφα	εἴλημμαι	ἐλήμφθην
convict	ἐλέγχω	ἐλέγξω	ἤλεγξα	———	ἐλήλεγμαι	ἠλέγχθην
say	λέγω	ἐρῶ	εἶπον	εἴρηκα	εἴρημαι	ἐρρήθην
leave	λείπω	λείψω	ἔλιπον	λέλοιπα	λέλειμμαι	ἐλείφθην
pity	ἐλεέω	ἐλεήσω	ἠλέησα	ἠλέηκα	ἠλέημαι	ἠλεήθην
reckon	λογίζομαι	λογιοῦμαι	ἐλογισάμην	———	λελόγισμαι	ἐλογίσθην
hope	ἐλπίζω	ἐλπιῶ	ἤλπισα	ἤλπισα	ἤλπικα	ἠλπίσθην
give pain to	λυπέω	λυπήσω	ἐλύπησα	λελύπηκα	———	ἐλυπήθην
loose	λύω	λύσω	ἔλυσα	λέλυκα	λέλυμαι	ἐλύθην
sin	ἁμαρτάνω	ἁμαρτήσω	ἥμαρτησα	ἡμάρτηκα	ἡμάρτημαι	ἡμαρτήθην
testify	μαρτυρέω	μαρτυρήσω	ἐμαρτύρησα	μεμαρτύρηκα	μεμαρτύρημαι	ἐμαρτυρήθην
divide	μερίζω	μεριῶ	ἐμέρισα	μεμέρικα	μεμέρισμαι	ἐμερίσθην
remember	μιμέομαι	μιμήσομαι	ἐμιμησάμην	———	μέμνημαι	ἐμνήσθην
hate	μισέω	μισήσω	ἐμίσησα	μεμίσηκα	μεμίσημαι	ἐμισήθην
swear	ὀμνύω	ὀμόσω	ὤμοσα	ὀμώμοκα	ὀμώμομαι	ὠμόσθην
do adultery	μοιχεύω	μοιχεύσω	ἐμοίχευσα	———	———	ἐμοιχεύθην
confess	ὁμολογέω	ὁμολογήσω	ὡμολόγησα	ὡμολόγηκα	ὡμολόγημαι	ὡμολογήθην
announce	ἀναγγέλλω	ἀναγγελῶ	ἀνήγγειλα	ἀνήγγελκα	ἀνήγγελμαι	ἀνηγγέλην
put on	ἐνδύω	ἐνδύσομαι	ἐνεδυσάμην	ἐνδέδυκα	ἐνδέδυμαι	ἐνεδύθην
revile	ὀνειδίζω	ὀνειδιῶ	ὠνείδισα	ὠνείδικα	———	ὠνειδίσθην
overcome	νικάω	νικήσω	ἐνίκησα	νενίκηκα	———	ἐνικήθην
open	ἀνοίγω	ἀνοίξω	ἀνέωξα	ἀνλεωγα	ἀνέωγμαι	ἀνεώχθην
name	ὀνομάζω	ὀνομάσω	ὠνόμασα	ὠνόμακα	ὠνόμασμαι	ὠνομάσθην
suppose	νομίζω	νομιῶ	ἐνόμισα	νενόμικα	νενόμισμαι	ἐνομίσθην
dry up	ξηραίνω	ξηρανῶ	ἐξήρανα	———	ἐξήρασμαι	ἐξηράνθην
build	οἰκοδομέω	οἰκοδομήσω	ᾠκοδόμησα	———	ᾠκοδόμημαι	οἰκοδομήθην
instruct	παιδεύω	παιδεύσω	ἐπαίδευσα	πεπαίδευκα	πεπαίδευμαι	ἐπαιδεύθην
strike	πατάσσω	πατάξω	ἐπάταξα	———	πεπάταγμαι	ἐπατάχθην
stop	παύω	παύσω	ἔπαυσα	πέπαυκα	πέπαυμαι	ἐπαύθην
persuade	πείθω	πείσω	ἔπεισα	πέποιθα	πέπεισμαι	ἐπείσθην
tempt	πειράζω	πειράσω	ἐπείρασα	πεπείρακα	πεπείρασμαι	ἐπειράσθην
fill	πίμπλημι	πλήσω	ἔπλησα	πέπληκα	πέπλησμαι	ἐπλήσθην
drink	πίνω	πίομαι	ἔπιον	πέπωκα	πέπομαι	ἐπόθην
believe	πιστεύω	πιστεύσω	ἐπίστευσα	πεπίστευκα	πεπίστευμαι	ἐπιστεύθην
mislead	πλανάω	πλανήσω	ἐπλάνησα	———	πεπλάνημαι	ἐπλανήθην
make full	πληρόω	πληρώσω	ἐπλήρωσα	πεπλήρωκα	πεπλήρωμαι	ἐπληρώθην
wash	πλύνω	πλυνῶ	ἔπλυνα	———	πέπλυμαι	———
make rich	πλουτίζω	πλουτίσω	ἐπλούτισα	πεπλούτικα	———	ἐπλουτίσθην
send	πέμπω	πέμψω	ἔπεμψα	πέπομφα	πέπεμμαι	ἐπέμφθην
die	ἀποθνήσκω	ἀποθανοῦμαι	ἀπέθανον	ἀποτέθνηκα	———	———

182

do/make	ποιέω	ποιήσω	ἐποίησα	πεποίηκα	πεποίημαι	ἐποιήθην
reveal	ἀποκαλύπτω	ἀποκαλύψω	ἀπεκάλυψα	———	———	ἀπεκαλύφθην
make war	πολεμέω	πολεμήσω	ἐπολέμησα	πεπολέμηκα	πεπολέμημαι	ἐπολεμήθην
go	πορεύομαι	πορεύσομαι	ἐπορευσάμην	πεπόρευκα	πεπόρευμαι	ἐπορεύθην
send	ἀποστέλλω	ἀποστελῶ	ἀπέστειλα	ἀπέσταλκα	ἀπέσταλμαι	ἀπεστάλην
do	πράσσω	πράξω	ἔπραξα	πέπραχα	πέπραγμαι	ἐπράχθην
touch	ἅπτομαι	ἅψομαι	ἧψα	———	ἧμμαι	ἥφθην
inquire	πυνθάνομαι	πεύσομαι	ἐπυθόμην	———	πέπυσμαι	———
set on fire	πυρόω	πυρώσω	ἐπύρωσα	πεπύρωκα	πεπύρωμαι	ἐπυρώθην
sell	πωλέω	πωλήσω	ἐπώλησα	πεπώληκα	πεπώλημαι	ἐπωλήθην
work	ἐργάζομαι	ἐργάσομαι	ἠργασάμην	———	εἴργασμαι	εἰργάσθην
deny	ἀρνέομαι	ἀρνήσομαι	ἠρνησάμην	———	ἤρνημαι	ἠρνήθην
seize	ἁρπάζω	ἁρπάσω	ἥρπασα	ἥρπακα	ἥρπασμαι	ἡρπάσθην
rule	ἄρχω	ἄρξω	ἦρξα	ἦρχα	ἦργμαι	ἤρχθην
see	ὁράω	ὄψομαι	ὠψάμην	εἶδον	ἑώρακα	ἑώραμαι
ask	ἐρωτάω	ἐρωτήσω	ἠρώτησα	ἠρώτηκα	ἠρώτημαι	ἠρωτήθην
extinguish	σβέννυμι	σβέσω	ἔσβεσα	ἔσβηκα		ἐσβέσθην
shake	σείω	σείσω	ἔσεισα	σέσεικα	σέσεισμαι	ἐσείσθην
save	σῴζω	σώσω	ἔσωσα	σέσωκα	σέσωσμαι	ἐσώθην
eat	ἐσθίω	φαγόμαι	ἔφαγον	ἐδήδοκα	ἐδήδεσμαι	———
be silent	σιγάω	σιγήσω	ἐσίγησα	σεσίγηκα	σεσίγημαι	ἐσιγήθην
keep silent	σιωπάω	σιωπήσω	ἐσιώπησα	σεσιώπηκα	σεσιώπημαι	ἐσιωπήθην
sow	σπείρω	σπερῶ	ἔσπειρα	ἔσπαρκα	ἔσπαρμαι	ἐσπάρην
hasten	σπουδάζω	σπουδάσω	ἐσπούδασα	ἐσπούδακα	ἐσπούδασμαι	ἐσπουδάσθην
crucify	σταυρόω	σταυρώσω	ἐσταύρωσα	ἐσταύπωκα	ἐσταύρωμαι	ἐσταυρώθην
lack	ὑστερέω	ὑστερήσω	ὑστέρησα	ὑστέρηκα	ὑστέρημαι	ὑστερήθην
stand	ἵστημι	στήσω	ἔστησα	ἔστηκα	ἔστημαι	ἐστάθην
establish	στηρίζω	στηρίσω	ἐστήριξα	———	ἐστήριγμαι	ἐστηρίχθην
turn	στρέφω	στρέψω	ἔστρψα	ἔστροφα	ἔστραμμαι	ἐστράφην
murder	σφάζω	σφάξω	ἔσφαξα	———	ἔσφαγμαι	ἐσφάχθην
seal	σφραγίζω	σφραγίσω	ἐσφράγισα		ἐσφράγισμαι	ἐσφραγίσθην
divide	σχίζω	σχίσω	ἔσχισα		ἔσχισμαι	ἐσχίσθην
be strong	ἰσχύω	ἰσχύσω	ἴσχυσα	ἴσχυκα	———	ἰσχύθην
stir up	ταράσσω	ταράξω	ἐτάραξα	τετάραχα	τετάραγμαι	ἐταράχθην
set in order	τάσσω	τάξω	ἔταξα	τέταχα	τέταγμαι	ἐτάκθην
complete	τελειόω	τελειώσω	ἐτελείωσα	τετελείωκα	τετελείωμαι	ἐτελειώθην
come to an end	τελευτάω	τελευτήσω	ἐτελεύτησα	τετελεύτηκα	———	ἐτελευτήθην
finish	τελέω	τελέσω	ἐτέλεσα	τετέλεκα	τετέλεσμαι	ἐτελέσθην
keep	τηρέω	τηρήσω	ἐτήρησα	τετήρηκα	τετήρημαι	ἐτηρήθην
put	τίθημι	θήσω	ἔθηκα	τέθεικα	τέθειμαι	ἐτέθην
value	τιμάω	τιμήσω	ἐτίμησα	τετίμηκα	τετίμημαι	ἐτιμήθην
give birth to	τίκτω	τέξομαι	ἔτεκον	τέτοκα	———	ἐτέχθην

prepare	ἑτοιμάζω	ἑτοιμάσω	ἡτοίμασα	ἡτοίμακα	ἡτοίμασμαι	ἡτοιμάσθην
be brave	τολμάω	τολμήσω	ἐτόλμησα	τετόλμηκα	———	———
nourish	τρέφω	θρέψω	ἔθρεψα	τέτροφα	τέθραμμαι	ἐτράφην
run	τρέχω	δραμοῦμαι	ἔδραμον	δεδράμηκα	δεδράμημαι	———
happen to be	τυγχάνω	τεύξομαι	ἔτυχον	τέτευχα	τέτευγμαι	ἐτεύχθην
strike	τύπτω	τύψω	ἔτυψα	τέτυψα	———	ἐτύφθην
to blind	τυφλόω	τυφλώσω	ἐτύφλωσα	τετύφλωκα	———	ἐτυφλώθην
shine	φαίνω	φανῶ	ἔφανα	πέφαγκα	πέφασμαι	ἐφάνθην
reveal	φανερόω	φανερώσω	ἐφανέρωσα	πεφανέρωκα	πεφανέρωμαι	ἐφανερώθην
owe	ὀφείλω	ὀφειλήσω	ὠφείλησα	ὠφείληκα	———	ὠφειλήθην
help	ὠφελέω	ὠφελήσω	ὠφέλησα	ὠφέληκα	ὠφέλημαι	ὠφελήθην
forgive	ἀφίημι	ἀφήσω	ἀφῆκα	ἀφεῖκα	ἀφέωμαι	ἀφέθην
love	φιλέω	φιλήσω	ἐφίλησα	πεφίληκα	———	ἐφιλήθην
fear	φοβέομαι	φοβήσω	ἐφόβησα	πεφόβηκα	πεφόβημαι	ἐφοβήθην
separate	ἀφοπίζω	ἀφορίσω	ἀφώρισα	———	ἀφώρισμαι	ἀφωπίσθην
close	φράσσω	φράξομαι	ἔφραξα	———	πέφραγμαι	ἐφράγην
carry	φέρω	οἴσω	ἤνεγκα	ἐνήνοχα	ἐνήνεγμαι	ἠνέχθην
guard	φυλάσσω	φυλάξω	ἐφύλαξα	πεφύλαχα	πεφύλαγμαι	ἐφυλάχθην
plant	φυτεύω	φυτεύσω	ἐφύτευσα	———	πεφύτευμαι	ἐφυτεύθην
illuminate	φωτίζω	φωτίσω	ἐφώτισα	πεφώτικα	πεφώτισμαι	ἐφωτίσθην
rejoice	χαίρω	χαρήσομαι	ἐχαρισάμην	———	κεχάρισμαι	ἐχάρην
give freely	χαρίζομαι	χαρίσομαι	ἐχαρισάμην	———	κεχάρισμαι	ἐχαρίσθην
impart	χηρματίζω	χηρματίσω	ἐχρημάτισα	κεχρημάτικα	κεχρημάτισμαι	ἐχρηματίσθην
make use of	χράομαι	-	ἐχρησάμην	———	κέχρημαι	ἐχρήσθην
anoint	χρίω	χρίσω	ἔχρισα	———	κέχρισμαι	ἐχρίσθην
have	ἔχω	ἕξω	ἔσχον	ἔσχηκα	ἔσχημαι	———
divide	χωρίζω	χωρίσω	ἐχώρισα	κεχώρισμαι	ἐχωρίσθην	———
lie	ψεύδομαι	ψεύσομαι	ἐψευσάμην	———	ἔψευσμαι	ἐψεύσθην
exalt	ὑψόω	ὑψώσω	ὕψωσα	ὕψωκα	———	ὑψώθην
permit	ἐάω	ἐάσω	εἴασα	εἴακα	———	ἐάθην

Printed in Great Britain
by Amazon

39840313R00112